INTERNATIONAL TRADE
THE BASICS

Trade impacts on the lives of all global citizens, influencing the range of commodities available for consumption and where those commodities are produced. Driven increasingly by market exchange, trade shapes the nature of work and how the costs and benefits of that work are distributed around the world. Economic growth and development are closely associated with the flows of goods and services between countries. *International Trade: The Basics* offers an accessible and engaging introduction to contemporary debates on international trade, inviting readers to explore the connections between national political economies within a globally integrated world.

Topics covered include:

- Why nations trade
- Globalization and transnational production networks
- Transnational governance
- The emergence of Asia as a major trade region
- Ethical trade and environmental sustainability
- Trade in solar energy, services and ideas.

Featuring case studies and social media links that help to illustrate key concepts, this book is an essential read for anyone seeking to understand how trade varies between regions, affects relationships between countries and influences a country's social, political and economic life.

Jessie Poon is Professor of Geography at the University of Buffalo-SUNY, USA. Her research interests are in the trade and investment activities of multinational firms. She has published over eighty articles and is editor of *Environment and Planning A*.

David L. Rigby is Professor of Geography at UCLA, USA with research interests in international trade, evolutionary economic geography, technological change and regional economic growth.

THE BASICS

For a full list of titles in this series, please visit www.routledge.com/The-Basics/book-series/B

INTERNATIONAL TRADE
THE BASICS

Jessie Poon and David L. Rigby

Routledge
Taylor & Francis Group

LONDON AND NEW YORK

First published 2017
by Routledge
2 Park Square, Milton Park, Abingdon, Oxon OX14 4RN

and by Routledge
711 Third Avenue, New York, NY 10017

Routledge is an imprint of the Taylor & Francis Group, an informa business

British Library Cataloguing in Publication Data
A catalogue record for this book is available from the British Library

Library of Congress Cataloging in Publication Data
Names: Poon, Jessie P. H., 1963– author. | Rigby, David L., author.
Title: International trade: the basics / Jessie Poon and David L. Rigby.
Description: Abingdon, Oxon; New York, NY: Routledge, 2017. | Includes bibliographical references and index.
Identifiers: LCCN 2016039172 | ISBN 9781138824386 (hardback) | ISBN 9781138824393 (pbk.) | ISBN 9781315740683 (ebook)
Subjects: LCSH: International trade.
Classification: LCC HF1379.P6635 2017 | DDC 382—dc23
LC record available at https://lccn.loc.gov/2016039172

ISBN: 978-1-138-82438-6 (hbk)
ISBN: 978-1-138-82439-3 (pbk)
ISBN: 978-1-315-74068-3 (ebk)

Typeset in Bembo
by Keystroke, Station Road, Codsall, Wolverhampton

CONTENTS

FIGURES

TABLES

BOXES

INTRODUCTION

Every four years, or so it seems, the population of the United States gets to revisit the concept of international trade. This is typically inspired by the presidential election cycle and whether the combatants are pro- or anti-trade. The frequency of such learning opportunities might be read as an index of the inability of US politicians to understand trade theory (likely, given the claims that are made), the importance of trade to US voters (also likely, given the growing complexity of the global economy) or perhaps both. Who could forget the arguments of Ross Perot, running as an independent in the 1992 presidential election contest and his claims of a "giant sucking sound", representing the movement of US jobs south of the border into Mexico that would follow passage of the North American Free Trade Agreement. In the current edition of this program we are reminded by Donald Trump that the US is a loser in terms of trade and that the only way to make the country "great again" is to allow him to renegotiate our trade deals with foreign partners. Meanwhile, Hilary Clinton and Bernie Sanders are battling over what kinds of trade agreements, if any, the United States should embrace. For them, the question is not that the US always loses through trade, but that the impacts of foreign trade are unevenly distributed across American workers. On the other side of the Atlantic, the benefits of trade are also being questioned as the UK voted to exit the European Union after decades of trade expansion with its continental neighbors. The so-called "Brexit" has generated great political and economic uncertainty and, perhaps, "the end of an era of transnational optimism" (Donadiojune, 2016).

What is trade, why do we trade and why do some groups rather than others benefit or lose as a result of trade? These are important questions that we explore throughout this book. Trade occurs when firms or consumers or even the government in one country purchase goods or services that are produced, in whole or in part, in other countries. The goods that we produce in the United States and sell in foreign markets are counted as US exports. The goods and services produced outside the US but purchased and consumed in this country are US imports. Firms and consumers in one part of the world purchase goods and services made elsewhere for a number of reasons. Perhaps the most obvious of these is that some commodities cannot be produced in all places. Certain fruits or vegetables can be grown only in locations with specific climate conditions. Other commodities require particular skills for their production that are found in relatively few countries. Advanced biotechnology products, for example, may be produced only in those places where workers and firms have the necessary capabilities or expertise. Yet, these firms produce drugs and medicines that can save lives across the world as a whole. In another case, consumers in one country might prefer a brand of automobile made in another country. Trade allows the consumer's love of variety to be satisfied. Finally, some countries are much more efficient than others at producing certain types of commodities. By exploiting variations in relative efficiency for different goods in different countries, trading partners might all benefit from trade.

If trade is beneficial for trading partners, then why are so many people angry about the impacts of trade? There are a number of answers to this question. First, even though free trade generates economic gains, how those gains are distributed is important. By altering international commodity prices, some countries might be able to capture more of the gains than others. Second, there are costs to trade as well as benefits. For example, when a high-wage economy such as France imports goods made by low-wage workers in the rest of the world, low-wage workers in France face lower wages and potential job-loss. At the same time, high-wage workers in France might see their wages increase as a result of international market integration. For France as a whole, trade might mean a reduction in the price of many goods, but this is little solace for workers who lose their jobs to rising imports. Third, by fueling growth, trade is often linked to environmental pollution and climate change. Many who protest trade are focused on the negative consequences of production within the market system. Finally, some protest trade because they may not understand the complexity of production networks that link various countries. Thus, when a country such as the United States is running a trade deficit, a higher value of imports relative to exports, some will complain about the unfair nature of global trade, or about one-sided trade deals that hurt US labor. The usual refrain is to "buy American". However, what many do not realize is that in today's global economy, many "American" firms have shifted production out of the US only to set up factories in foreign locations. Thus, many of the imports that drive the US trade deficit are commodities made by US firms in other countries. It is not clear that moving such production back to the US would generate net benefits for the US economy. Let us briefly explore the case of Apple and production of the iPhone.

Apple's iPhone is a commodity produced by workers spread across many countries of the world. The iPhone design and iOS software are developed at Apple's headquarters in Cupertino, California. Key components of the iPhone are sourced from other firms in the United States, Europe and East Asia. All these components are assembled into the iPhone in the Chinese factories of the Taiwanese electronics firm Hon Hai Precision Industry, better known to many by the trade name Foxconn. It is estimated that Apple employs about 110,000 workers around the world, approximately 40% of that number in retail activities, with about the same proportion of its overall work-force located outside the United States. Duhigg and Bradsher (2012) of the *New York Times* suggested that approximately 700,000 people develop and assemble Apple products in firms linked to Apple through contracting and sub-contracting relationships around the world. Indeed, Foxconn employs over 1 million workers at its Chinese factories alone. Though the number of Foxconn workers employed directly on the iPhone is unknown, estimates put that number at well over 300,000.

The iPhone is a classic example of what we imagine as a "global commodity", a product designed, manufactured and assembled in different parts of the world before being sold almost everywhere. Why did Apple adopt this global style of organizing its operations as opposed to producing the iPhone exclusively in the United States? The answer is that it is much more cost effective for Apple to exploit international variations in skills and prices of inputs, especially labor, than to produce its products in a single country, even after the cost of transportation is factored in. Most of the jobs associated with iPhone production are those that involve the assembly of components into the finished product. These jobs are relatively low-skilled and thus it makes sense for Apple to locate such production in emerging economies like China, where low-skilled workers are abundant and paid relatively low wages. But this is not the whole story. It is widely acknowledged that few countries can match the manufacturing flexibility of the Chinese economy. With vast numbers of workers distributed across different kinds of manufacturing operations, China offers advantages to firms operating at many different points along the supply chains (the networks of firms) that produce so much of the world's output.

How does the production activity of a corporation like Apple impact trade? Many iPhones, once assembled, are shipped from China to the United States and to other countries around the world. These shipments represent exports from China and imports to the countries where they end their journey. In 2009, the value of iPhone exports from China to the United States was estimated at US$1.9 billion (Xing and Detert, 2010), contributing significantly to the US trade deficit with China. Thus, buying a smartphone from a US corporation like Apple would not help the US trade deficit and it might generate more jobs in foreign countries than in the United States. Most all trade economists would still insist that this global organization of production is a net positive for the US economy, and that it is not in the country's best interests for the jobs in the Foxconn plants within China to return to this country. Low-wage workers in the US are likely to dispute these claims, and environmentalists might argue that there are additional costs to trade. While the net effect of Apple's imports is still being debated, what seems clear is that trade has grown exponentially in the past few decades, driven by the global activities of companies like Apple.

THE GROWTH OF TRADE

Figure 1.1 maps the ratio of trade ((imports + exports)/2) to gross domestic product (GDP) for the world economy since 1870. GDP measures the total value of goods and services produced within a given year (in this case for all countries in the world). The trade to GDP ratio is a common index of the importance of trade for an individual country or for the world as a whole.

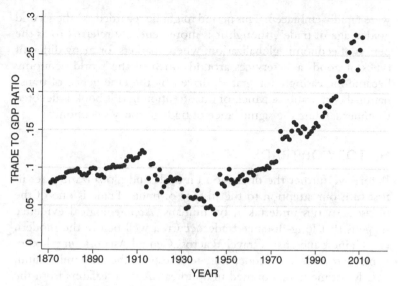

Figure 1.1 Growth of world trade, 1870–2010

Source: Penn World Tables 8.1 and Klasing and Milionis (2014)

Note: The trade to GDP ratio is measured as ((imports + exports)/2)/GDP.

The sharp rise in the significance of trade since 1950 or so is clearly illustrated in Figure 1.1. In that year the trade to GDP ratio was approximately 8.6%. By 1980 the trade to GDP ratio had reached 16.1%, and it climbed further, peaking at just under 28% in 2008. Figure 1.1 illustrates what has become known as the "first golden age of trade" which occupied the years between 1890 and 1913. This period was marked by a rapid opening of international borders to flows of goods, capital and people, stimulated in part by improvements in transportation technology. This golden age ended abruptly with the onset of the First World War. The decline in trade continued through the interwar years pushed deeper by the Great Depression and increases in tariffs (taxes on the international movement of goods) that became a common policy response to economic decline.

After the Second World War, under the impetus of the General Agreement on Tariffs and Trade (GATT), tariffs around the world gradually fell, new transportation technologies such as containerization emerged and new "global" forms of commodity production were rapidly embraced. This period might be regarded as "the second golden age of trade", though it is more generally referred to as the period of economic globalization, where markets for many different types of goods and services around much of the world economy became increasingly integrated, driven by the emergence of trans-national corporations. Much of our attention in this book is devoted to understanding the significance of trade in today's economy.

HISTORY OF TRADE

Before we further the discussion on trade and globalization, let us first turn our attention to the history of trade. Trade is one of the oldest activities undertaken by humans. Archaeological evidence suggests that long-distance trade occurred well before the modern era. Chinese merchants traveled across Central Asia bringing luxury items such as silk and lacquer ware to Europe in the third millennium BCE. Maritime trade boomed in Southeast Asia as seafarers from the Middle East, India and China engaged in exchanges of cotton (India), sugar (Philippines), tin (Malaysia), spices (Indonesia) and tea and silk (China) destined for Europe (Lockard, 2009). Both the Indian Ocean and South China Sea became hubs of the medieval world's most important maritime trade networks between the tenth and fifteenth centuries. Indeed, Asia was the center of trade exchanges during this period so much so that it attracted Europeans like the Portuguese to set up forts at Malacca (Malaysia) and Hormus (Iran) to control shipping routes across the Indian Ocean in a bid for a share of the trade activities here.

It was the industrial revolution of the eighteenth and nineteenth centuries that unleashed historic transformations in Europe and later in North America, and these in turn affected trade permanently. The revolution created durable industrial structures and forms of economic organization for long-distance trade that established the international trade economy that we know today. The modern factory began in eighteenth-century England with the textile revolution and industrial production of cloth. Long a small-scale, cottage industry based largely on wool, cloth production moved into large-scale mills following the introduction of a series of new weaving technologies that rapidly increased the demand for yarn. A switch from wool to stronger cotton fibers fueled the growth of factory production assisted by the British

Calico Acts, tariffs on the import of cotton fabrics (largely from India) put in place to protect the domestic British textile industry. In place of cotton fabrics, raw cotton was imported from British colonies, at first India, but then the Americas. As the scale of cotton production expanded, new mechanized spinning and weaving technologies were developed that allowed Britain to establish a position as the world's most efficient producer of cotton goods. India, once the primary source of imported cotton fabrics to England, now became a major market for British cotton exports.

The growth of the textile sector in Britain stimulated the expansion of related industries. Firms producing industrial machinery developed to support the growth of manufacturing, while many other firms emerged to serve an expanding population of consumers demanding a greater variety of commodities from the rest of the world. All this required imports of raw materials: for example, copper from California, used to make electrical wires. Agricultural trade also became more important. Drinking tea in Britain became a fashionable social activity and most of that tea was imported from South Asia, along with sugar from the Philippines and South America. In other words, trade was central to industrial revolution in the UK, linking this economy to the geographical division of labor that was unfolding in order to support international trade.

As the industrial revolution spread to other parts of Europe, demand for agricultural and raw materials expanded. Unable to compete with England for India's cotton and other raw materials from the country's colonies, European countries began to search elsewhere. The era of colonialism is often associated with Europe's search for raw materials to fuel its factories and industrial growth. It is also associated with the rise of an international economy. By this, we mean that trade in the eighteenth and nineteenth centuries facilitated more durable linkages and interconnectedness between countries, and that contact strengthened economic relations. Having previously supplied cotton and sugar to Europe, the United States soon joined the industrial revolution. Major American industrial barons like John Rockefeller formed alliances with railroad and freight companies to develop a transportation system that would facilitate the export of oil, first from Pennsylvania to the rest of the country, and then to the rest of the world, building one of the country's largest vertically integrated companies, Standard Oil (ExxonMobil today). In so doing, he helped transform the Northeast of the United States into an industrial powerhouse and trade center, served by an extensive network of transportation that ensured the uninterrupted shipment and export of commodities around the world.

Historians associate the spread of colonial trade during the industrial revolution to the change in technology from the invention of the steam engine that allowed ships and trains to ferry cargo across great distances, to the telegraph and telephone that enhanced information flows among trading houses. Such inventions signal a trend of technological progress that trade carried around the globe. Shipping goods great distances was possible because of the cumulative inventions of a number of technicians and scientists in Britain and continental Europe. For instance, Joseph Black's theory of latent heat inspired James Watt to build a separate condenser that resulted in a more efficient steam engine. Installing the steam engine in ships meant that merchants could sail across the Atlantic Ocean in a week, speeding the movement of cargo. Britain's precociousness in trade during this period was in part linked to the country's successful application of new techniques that fuelled the industrial revolution (Mokyr, 2002). This in turn encouraged national and regional specialization that deepened the spatial division of labor between Britain (as producer of capital and consumer goods) and its colonies (as suppliers of raw materials).

Colonial trade was vital to Europe's industrial modernization. Until then, trade bustled across the Mediterranean Sea, the Indian Ocean and South China Sea so much that the historical geographer Reid (1988) conferred the "Age of commerce" on Southeast Asia in the 300 years prior to the eighteenth century. Trade's impact then was visible through the growth of cities. As centers of innovation, urban growth was partially explained by the number of port cities that sprang up to support maritime trade. The impacts of trade may be traced by levels of urbanization across Asia. India and China, for instance, had a higher urbanization rate at around 11% compared to levels near 8.5% in Western Europe around 1400 (Acemoglu et al., 2005). As the industrial revolution gathered force, Atlantic trade began to increase markedly. Acemoglu and his colleagues show that the center of trading activities shifted to the Atlantic Ocean during this period. In turn, rates of urbanization across European countries like Britain, France, the Netherlands, Portugal and Spain also increased sharply. By the mid-nineteenth century, the urbaniza-tion level of these countries had surpassed Asia to reach nearly 20%. Income levels rose rapidly with trade and urbanization across much of Western Europe, while they stagnated across Asia. The rise of modern Western Europe is closely intertwined with the rise of the Atlantic trade.

From the discussion above, an emerging international economy was clearly beginning to blossom by the end of the nineteenth century, with increasing numbers of countries connected through trade. Within many national economies, trade helped forge new social classes (merchants), becoming a major instrument of wealth. Trade also shaped new institutions that contributed to market stabil-ity. In these different ways, trade is generally seen as a positive force for national and regional economic growth. However, it is important to note that much of the history of international trade is not charac-terized by free trade (Bairoch, 1993). Battling with Adam Smith and David Ricardo were those who argued for greater protection of industries from foreign competition in order to build stronger domestic economies. Friedrich List (1789–1846) was a champion of tariffs to stimulate domestic economic activity. Another example of protectionism is England's famous 1815 Corn Laws established to ban the import of wheat until domestic prices rose to a desirable level. In this way the Corn Laws protected the wealth of the landown-ing class. Although England briefly became one of the most liberal economies in the mid-1800s, this was not the case on continental Europe where manufacturers remained unconvinced of the merits of free trade for much of the colonial era.

Trade could not have expanded at such a rapid rate in the colonial era without institutional support. The development of a parliamen-tary system and robust financial support through the Bank of England coupled with the decline in the power of the monarchy in England increased merchants' freedom to trade across the Atlantic without being unduly beholden to royal interests. From a governance per-spective, institutions that support property rights and that help to ensure certainty in economic exchanges are necessary for trade to flourish. Western European countries that underwent institutional transformation saw substantial gains in trade and economic growth (Acemoglu et al., 2005). In the contemporary context, trade govern-ance is one of the most internationalized activities in the context of institution-building. There are not many truly global institutions where so many countries (about 162 in 2015) have agreed to participate in multilateral transactions. In trade, we find one of the most powerful global institutions set up primarily to enhance property rights, to minimize protectionism and to establish mechanisms for the settling of disputes between countries through the World Trade Organization or WTO (see Chapter 4). To understand why trade governance has become so global, we describe prevailing trade patterns in the next section.

GLOBALIZATION AND CONTEMPORARY TRADE PATTERNS

Based on World Bank data, and summing imports and exports to generate a total trade value, more than 161 countries around the world posted a trade to GDP ratio greater than 50% in 2008. While the figure of 50% is a somewhat arbitrary threshold, and Chapter 3 illustrates some problems with this kind of measure, never before have so many countries engaged in this level of trade. The world economy is dramatically more connected today than at any other time.

Figure 1.2 maps the global flow of commodities traced by international trade data in 2014. According to the United Nations, the value of world merchandise trade (the average of imports and exports) in 2014 was approximately US$18,000 billion. (All dollar figures throughout this book will refer to US dollars.) Trade in services is not included in this total as imports and exports of services are not tracked as reliably as trade in goods. Each of the major world regions indicated in Figure 1.2 contains a number of countries that trade with one another and with countries that belong to other major regions. Examining the volume of trade that takes place within each of these major regions, it is clear that intra-European trade dominates the global flow of goods, comprising around 25% of all world merchandise trade. Trade within Asia makes up the second most important intra-regional flow, accounting for approximately 11% of world trade. North American trade flows are dominated by exchanges between Canada and the US, and these make up only about 4% of world trade. (Note that Mexico is included in Latin America in Figure 1.2.)

Turning to flows between the major world regions, Figure 1.2 indicates that the largest volume of inter-regional trade occurs

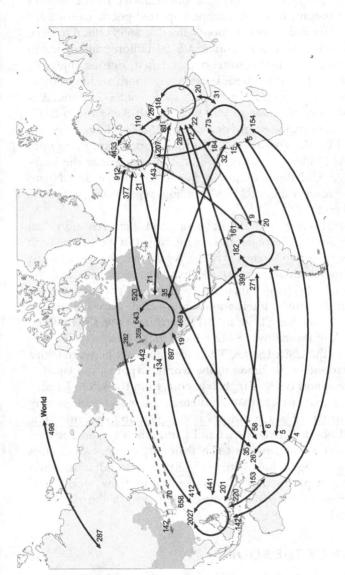

Figure 1.2 Map of world trade, 2014

Source: UN Comtrade

Notes: Trade flows of goods are shown for 2014 in billions of US dollars. World trade in goods in 2014 was approximately $18,000 billion. The circular lines show trade flows within major regions (Asia, Oceania, North America, Latin America, Europe, Africa and the Middle-East). The curved solid lines show imports and exports between major world regions, while the dashed lines show imports and exports between Canada and the US, between China and the US and between Japan and the US.

between Asia, Europe and North America. This is not surprising as these regions produce and consume the majority of the world's merchandise output. In 2014, Europe imported goods worth $912 billion from Asia and exported goods valued at $658 billion to Asia. This means that Europe was running a $254 billion trade deficit in goods with Asia. Countering some of that deficit, Europe enjoyed a trade surplus with North America, exporting goods with a value of $520 billion while importing goods with a value of $377 billion. Asia also enjoyed a sizeable trade surplus with North America. In 2014, Asian economies exported goods valued at $897 billion to North America, while the countries of North America exported goods valued at $412 billion to Asian nations. Adding together the intra- and inter-regional flows of goods for Asia, Europe and North America, we reach a sum of $10,879 billion, representing over 60% of all world trade.

There are also large bilateral flows of goods between individual countries. Figure 1.2 illustrates some of the largest of these flows with dashed lines. The two countries of the world that share the largest volume of merchandise imports and exports are Canada and the United States. In 2014, more than $641 billion worth of goods crossed the US–Canada border. International goods trade between the US and China was also very large in 2014, totaling some $583 billion. The vast bulk of those flows, $442 billion, took the form of exports from China to the United States. The trade imbalance between China and the US is one of the largest in the world. Exports from Japan to the US were almost twice as high as exports from the US to Japan.

Figure 1.2 makes clear that the volume of world trade is very large. The structure of trade flows is complex and dynamic. The exchange of goods between Asia and Latin America and between Asia and Africa is much greater today than only one or two decades earlier. These changes, along with many others, reflect dramatic shifts in the way that production is organized around the world. The increased levels of international integration are a hallmark of our global economy.

OBJECTIVE OF THE BOOK

In the Apple story above, who wins and who loses? This depends on how we understand the objectives, functions and broad impacts of trade. From an economic viewpoint, a seamless or borderless world of commodity exchanges between countries is good for the global economy because consumers benefit from a greater variety of goods and services, often at low prices, producers of export goods are exposed to wider markets, and companies need only produce goods and services that reflect their opportunity costs. However, as pointed out above, free trade is not without costs and these costs may be distributed unevenly. The job of the nation-state is not simply to ensure that markets operate fairly. Nation-states should be concerned about the costs of trade as well as the benefits and should set policy to try and balance the interests of competing groups.

In reality, trade does not operate seamlessly across the global economy. Government officials must worry about import competition and product dumping, and about job creation and job loss across regions and sectors of the economy. They must also worry about the fallout of trade from polluting industries. Different groups within countries lobby the government to increase trade, to slow it down or even halt it. At times business may be pro-trade and workers against it. At other times, firms and labor unions may join forces to fight foreign competition by demanding increases in tariffs or non-tariff trade barriers. Imports are also limited through place-specific cultural practices (e.g. Japanese keiretsu networks) that encourage companies to source from domestic producers. That economic, political and cultural factors are relevant in understanding why trade occurs and the form that trade takes in different parts of the global economy suggests that an inter-disciplinary approach to make sense of the flow of goods and services around the world is required. This book attempts to provide such an approach.

OUTLINE OF THE BOOK

In Chapter 2 of this book, we outline the classical theory of free trade, we explore the factors that influence who gains from trade, and we extend trade theory to account for trade between countries that produce similar commodities and to explain patterns of foreign outsourcing in the contemporary global economy. Chapter 3 explores the emergence and growth of the global economy and trade through the activities of transnational corporations and their development of their production networks. In Chapter 4, the governance of trade is examined and the nature of economic integration and trade agreements in different parts of the world economy is detailed. Chapter 5 turns to explore the connections between trade and development. Specifically, it elaborates the trade strategies of developing countries with a focus on East and Southeast Asia. In Chapter 6 we examine the impacts of trade, from the development of export processing zones, through to the influence of trade on labor and the environment. We push the discussion further, analyzing the growing demand for ethical forms of trade. Chapter 7 offers a brief conclusion summarizing our main arguments and highlighting a series of future trade-related concerns.

SUGGESTED READING

Bairoch, P. (1993) *Economics and World History*. Chicago: University of Chicago Press.

The book traces the relationship between free trade and economic growth in the nineteenth century. It is an interesting read with Bairoch generating some controversial statements. For example, he suggested that Britain and continental Europe's reduction of protectionism slowed their growth, and that colonialism was not exploitative because developing countries were not central to the economic development of Western industrialized countries. It is a short book and contains historical data.

Reid, A. (1988) *Southeast Asia in the Age of Commerce, 1450 to 1680*. New Haven, CT: Yale University Press.

The world experienced periods of globalization before the industrial revolution, as Reid demonstrates in this book on Southeast Asia. China and Southeast Asia had long engaged in sea-going trade. Reid's attention to the period of 1450–1680 shows how such trade transformed Southeast Asia in the political and religious context from one of integration to the world economy to one of withdrawal from trade by the end of the 1600s.

RESOURCES

The Apple supplier list and map of production may be examined at:

http://www.apple.com/supplier-responsibility/our-suppliers/ and http://comparecamp.com/how-where-iphone-is-made-comparison-of-apples-manufacturing-process/

A teardown sheet for the Apple iPhone 6, and many other commodities may be found at http://www.techinsights.com/teardown.com/apple-iphone-6/

The Penn World Tables provide data on trade and GDP for many countries around the world: http://cid.econ.ucdavis.edu/pwt.html

The United Nations Conference on Trade and Development provides additional sources of trade data through its UN Comtrade site http://comtrade.un.org/ and through the United Nations Conference on Trade and Development http://unctad.org/

The World Bank is another source of international economic data: http://data.worldbank.org/

2

TRADE THEORY

In Chapter 1 we illustrated the rising importance of trade within the world economy. Increases in the ratio of imports or exports to gross domestic product (GDP) are common to many countries, especially over the past fifty years or so. Yet, the expansion of trade is not universally supported. Some fear that trade is to blame for job losses and stagnant wages in both advanced industrialized nations as well as emerging economies. Others suggest that trade might damage the growth prospects of developing nations as a whole. And, there are mounting concerns about the influence of trade on food security and the environment. If trade is so bad, why do most countries actively support the exchange of goods and services across their borders? The simple reason is that there are gains from trade. From the ability to access a greater variety of goods and services, to the more efficient utilization of a country's resources, the benefits of free trade (trade that is not restricted by taxes or other forms of regulation on imports or exports) often outweigh the costs of opening an economy to international competition.

While it is relatively easy to show the existence of gains from trade, how those gains are distributed between countries and across different groups within countries is a more complicated question. The aim of this chapter is to explore different theories of international trade, to show how the economic gains from trade are generated and to discuss the factors that influence who captures those gains. We open the discussion with the standard introduction to trade in the form of a model of comparative advantage. Our understanding of trade is extended by investigating the distribution of trade benefits within countries via the Heckscher–Ohlin (H-O) theorem. Models of international trade that rest upon the framework of monopolistic competition are introduced next. These models help us understand why countries that produce similar products trade with one another. A new basis for trade in the form of global outsourcing ends our overview of trade theory. The discussion ends with a brief summary of key points.

COMPARATIVE ADVANTAGE

The early case for the benefits of trade was outlined by Adam Smith in the late eighteenth century and by David Ricardo in the early nineteenth century. At the time, it was widely considered that wealth takes the form of gold and silver and thus that nation-states should engage in international trade only insofar as it increased their accumulation of these resources. This was the view of **mercantilism** and it led to policy that limited imports (and thus the loss of gold and silver to pay for goods purchased from foreign countries) while encouraging exports. Early political struggles over free trade, the removal of legislation setting quotas and **tariffs** (taxes on goods crossing national borders), primarily on imports, are explored by Sheppard (2005).

In *The Wealth of Nations* (1776), Adam Smith explored the bases of competition and economic growth, arguing that a nation's **resources** (raw materials, land, labor and capital) should be used to produce only those commodities that the nation is efficient at supplying. If foreign countries could produce other commodities more efficiently than the nation being considered, then he reasoned those other commodities should be imported. What does Smith mean in terms of efficiency? To answer this question, let us assume that there are only two countries, A and B, that both these countries produce only two goods, wine and cloth, and that the production process is very simple using a single input, labor.

With labor as the only input used to produce wine and cloth, the efficiency of the production process is measured by **labor productivity**, the number of units of wine or cloth produced on average by one worker employed for a fixed unit of time, say an hour or a day. A simple example serves to clarify this meaning of efficiency. In country A on average, one day of labor can produce 4 units of wine or 1 unit of cloth. In country B on average, one day of labor can produce 2 units of wine or 3 units of cloth. Thus, we say that country A has an **absolute advantage** over country B in producing wine, because one unit of labor can produce more wine in country A than in country B. Similarly, country B has an absolute advantage over country A in the production of cloth.

With no trade, if we assume that residents of both countries demand 60 units of wine and 60 units of cloth each day, this means 60/4 = 15 workers will be needed in country A to produce wine and 60/1 = 60 workers will be needed to produce cloth. In country B, the daily labor requirements will be 30 wine workers and 20 cloth workers. Now assume that country A and country B can trade with one another. We keep things simple at first by assuming that **trade costs**, the costs of moving goods from one country to the other, are zero. Perhaps the two countries are neighbors! After some experimentation it should become clear that our two countries can benefit from trade if they each specialize in producing that commodity in which they have an absolute advantage. For example, if country A takes all its 75 workers and uses them to produce wine, the daily output would be equal to 75*4 = 300 units of wine. If country B specializes in cloth production, it could produce each day 50*3 = 150 units of cloth. After specializing, total output across our two countries has increased by 180 units of wine and 30 units of cloth. If shared between the two countries, this additional output represents the **gains from trade**.

While Smith's model of absolute advantage establishes the possibility of gains from trade, those possibilities arise only when different countries each possess absolute advantage in the production of at least one commodity. In this respect, Smith's model provides a rather limited basis for trade: there are many countries that engage in trade that likely have no absolute advantages over the rest of the world. What drives these countries to trade? The answer rests on the concept of **comparative advantage** outlined by David Ricardo in his 1817 book *On the Principles of Political Economy and Taxation*.

We develop the arguments of comparative advantage using the same two-country, two-commodity, one-input model introduced above. Note how labor productivity is adjusted in this new model. To begin, let us imagine that there is no trade, a situation of **autarky**, between the two countries A and B. In this pre-trade world we assume that country A uses its labor to make wine and cloth. The amount of wine and cloth that country A can produce depends on the productivity of labor in the wine and cloth industries and on the total supply of labor that is fixed at 100 workers, or more precisely, 100 worker-days. The productivity of labor in the wine industry of country A is assumed to be $100/100 = 1$. That is, if all 100 workers in country A produced wine and no cloth they could produce 100 units of wine. The productivity of labor in the cloth industry of country A is also set at $100/100 = 1$. Thus, if all the workers in country A specialized in producing cloth, they could produce 100 units in a single day. These production possibilities are mapped in panel a of Figure 2.1 in the form of a **production possibilities frontier** (PPF). The PPF maps all possible combinations of wine and cloth that might be produced using the available labor in a country. Note that complete specialization in Figure 2.1 means that only one of the two commodities is produced in a country. Specialization is captured by the ends of the PPF where they cross the horizontal and vertical axes.

To draw the PPF for a country we divide the nation's labor supply by the productivity of labor in wine production. This value fixes the point at which the PPF crosses the axis that measures the volume of wine produced. For country A this point is $100/1 = 100$, illustrated on the vertical axis in panel a. Next, we find the point where the PPF crosses the axis that measures the volume of cloth produced. For country A this value is also 100, shown on the horizontal axis in panel 1. The PPF is drawn by connecting these two points. The slope of the PPF represents the amount of wine that country A must give up in order to produce one more unit of cloth. The slope of the PPF is negative and its value (–1) is also referred to as the **opportunity cost** of producing cloth. The opportunity cost for producing one more unit of a good within a country is the amount of production in the other good that must be foregone.

In country B, we assume that the reserves of labor are set at 100 workers, the same as in country A. Country B is given a different **technology** than country A. This means wine and cloth are produced in country B with different amounts of labor than in A. The productivity of labor in wine production in country B is assumed to be $90/100 = 0.9$ and the productivity of labor in cloth production is $30/100 = 0.3$. The PPF for country B in the pre-trade scenario is shown in panel b of Figure 2.1. With its 100 units of labor, the PPF reveals that country B could produce either 90 units of wine or 30 units of cloth or any combination of wine and cloth on the straight-line between these points. The slope of the PPF in country B is -3. Thus, the opportunity cost of cloth production in country B is 3 units of wine. This value can be considered as the **relative price** of 1 unit of cloth, a figure that reflects the relative amount of labor used in the production of both goods. The reciprocal of this value represents the price of 1 unit of wine relative to cloth (1/3).

Where exactly do countries locate on their PPF? This depends on the level of demand for our two commodities within each country. We can represent that demand with **indifference curves**. An indifference curve traces different combinations of goods the consumption of which generates equal levels of satisfaction or utility for individuals, or in aggregate for an economy. A family of indifference curves represents different levels of utility, those closer to the origin measuring lower levels of utility than those further away. If we assume that individuals seek higher rather than lower utility then they will choose to consume along the indifference curve that is farthest from the origin. The indifference curve that is tangential to the PPF denotes the maximum level of consumption that is possible within an economy. In panel a of Figure 2.1 the highest indifference curve that is possible to reach is I_2^A. It is important to recognize that with no trade, consumption within a country is limited by the nation's production. A represents the point of production and consumption that maximizes utility in country A. At point A, production and consumption amount to 50 units of cloth and 50 units of wine. In panel b for country B, point B marks the location of highest utility in the pre-trade environment with production and consumption of 22 units of cloth and 24 units of wine.

Notice that in the pre-trade panels of Figure 2.1 country A has an absolute advantage in producing both wine and cloth relative to country B. This raises the question of whether country A would benefit from trade with country B; after all, it is more efficient at producing both goods. Ricardo's model of comparative advantage establishes that the answer to this question is yes, so long as the opportunity cost of producing wine relative to wheat varies between the two countries. It is then straightforward to show that free trade will generate gains for both countries if each of them specializes in producing the commodity where they hold the greatest comparative advantage, the commodity where their opportunity costs are minimized.

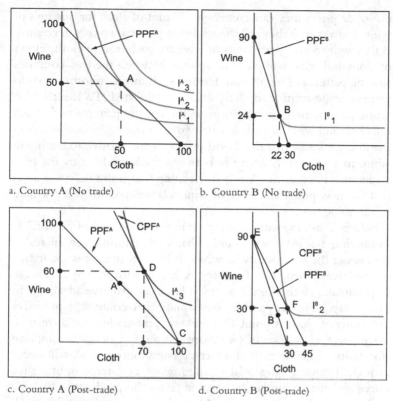

a. Country A (No trade)

b. Country B (No trade)

c. Country A (Post-trade)

d. Country B (Post-trade)

Figure 2.1 Illustration of comparative advantage

Assume that trade opens up between our two countries. As before, we assume that they are neighbors and thus transport costs are zero. When the flow of goods between countries is first allowed, the relative prices of our two commodities will vary inside each country; they will take time to adjust. Enterprising individuals will see these price differentials and attempt to profit from them in a process known as **arbitrage**, buying a commodity at a low price in one location and selling it for a higher price somewhere else. For example, one unit of cloth in country B might be exchanged for three units of wine. These three units of wine might then be moved to country A and exchanged for cloth such that a profit of two units of cloth is realized. Alternatively, producers of cloth in country A will recognize that at pre-trade prices they can exchange one unit of cloth for one unit of wine. However, if they sell their wine at pre-trade prices in country B they will receive three units of wine for each unit of cloth. Flows of cloth and wine will grow in volume between the two countries altering patterns of supply and demand such that a uniform or world price of wine relative to cloth will be established. To identify this world price requires information on the specific patterns of demand for cloth and wine in each of our two countries. Absent that information, we know that the world price of wine relative to cloth will adjust to a value somewhere in between the bounds set by the pre-trade price in countries A and B. Keeping things simple, we assume that the new post-trade price of wine relative to cloth will gravitate to the value two.

We establish the gains from trade in panels c and d of Figure 2.1. Following Ricardo, we assume that each country specializes in producing the commodity in which it has the greatest comparative (or relative) advantage. Country A has a comparative advantage in producing cloth while country B has a comparative advantage in producing wine. In panel c, we assume that country A produces 100 units of cloth at point C. The new post-trade (world) relative price line with a slope of two maps out a set of new consumption possibilities in country A. Post-trade consumption in A will occur at point D that is tangential to the highest post-trade indifference curve and that is physically possible given the production of wine and cloth in both economies. Note that, post-trade, within each country consumption and production may vary. At point D workers in country A consume 70 units of the cloth they produce while also consuming 60 units of wine. That wine is imported from country B in exchange for 30 units of cloth produced in country A and exported. In panel d, country B produces 90 units of wine at point E. With the new world relative price line, workers in country B consume 30 units of the wine they produce at point F, exporting the remaining 60 units of wine in return for 30 units of cloth from country A.

The gains from trade in country A are represented by the difference in consumption before and after trade. These gains are represented by the distance between points A and D in panel c of Figure 2.1. This distance is 20 units of cloth and 10 units of wine, representing the additional consumption in country A resulting from specialization and trade. In country B the gains from trade are represented by the distance between points B and F of panel d. This distance is 8 units of cloth and 6 units of wine. Both countries thus enjoy higher levels of consumption after trade.

Note that country A gains from trade with country B even though it is absolutely more efficient at producing both wine and cloth. Country A is relatively more efficient at producing cloth and country B is relatively more efficient at producing wine. These differences in relative efficiency dictate the patterns of specialization in the model of comparative advantage. It should be clear that comparative advantage offers a much broader base for trade than absolute advantage. Trading nations do not have to search for partners that are absolutely more efficient than they are in producing at least one commodity.

THE HECKSCHER–OHLIN MODEL

As we have just seen, variations in efficiency or technology between countries are one basis for trade. There are other foundations on which we can develop arguments to show the potential gains from trade. One of the most important of these alternatives is the uneven distribution of resources across countries. While the models of absolute advantage and comparative advantage are important, they are also quite limited in the sense that they consider simple production processes where there is only one input. This makes it impossible to examine whether or not the owners of different kinds of inputs within a country all gain from trade. In order to answer this question, we extend the two-country, two-commodity model of the last section by adding a second input, or **factor of production**, to our economies. In the first part of this section the impacts of a second factor of production on our model of trade are explored. In the second part of the section we discuss the arguments of Heckscher and Ohlin, two trade-economists writing early in the twentieth century, who explain the patterns of specialization in our new two-input world. We then follow Heckscher and Ohlin to show that within one country the owners of different inputs to production will not all gain from trade.

We set up our new model of trade assuming that a second input, land, is required to produce wine and cloth along with labor in our two countries A and B. Again we explore how production and consumption shift within and between these economies from a situation of autarky to one embracing international trade. With a second factor of production we are forced to think a little more carefully about the shape of the PPF. In the model of comparative advantage the PPF is a straight-line indicating that regardless of the level of output of the two commodities within one country, the productivity of labor (and the opportunity costs of production) remains unchanged. This is not a very realistic situation with a second factor of production. To see this, assume that each unit of wine produced within a country requires a lot of land and little labor, while each unit of cloth produced requires a lot of labor and little land. Wine production is said to be **land-intensive** and cloth production **labor-intensive**. In Figure 2.2 we illustrate the PPF for a country in our two-input world as a curve that is bowed-out or concave from the origin. The negative slope of the PPF denotes the fact that to produce more of one commodity means giving up some units of the second commodity, for inputs to production are finite or scarce. The curved shape of the PPF means that repeated increases of a given magnitude in the production of one good require larger and larger sacrifices in terms of reduced levels of production of the other good. This implies that the opportunity cost of each commodity increases as the volume of production of that commodity grows.

These changes in opportunity costs are sometimes referred to as the **law of increasing (relative) cost**. One simple explanation for the operation of this law is differences in the quality of the inputs to production. In our example this means that parcels of land may vary in their fertility and thus are more or less productive in terms of wine production, or that different workers are more or less productive in cloth or wine production. Thus, if we assume that the most fertile land is used for wine production rather than cloth production, when the economy desires more and more wine, greater amounts of increasingly less fertile land are required to sustain the additional demand for wine and that means larger and larger reductions in the amount of cloth that is produced. Figure 2.2 shows that the opportunity cost of cloth production increases with the volume of cloth made as shown by the slope of the PPF at points A, B and C.

Where on the PPF should the economy decide to produce in this new two-input environment? This depends on the country's demands for wine and cloth. As in the models of comparative advantage, if we

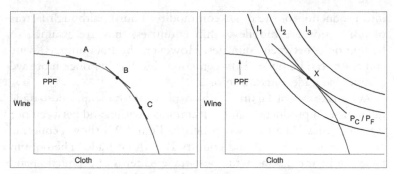

Figure 2.2 The production possibilities frontier with two inputs

represent that demand in the form of economy-wide indifference curves, then the economy should locate at that point on the PPF that is tangential to the highest indifference curve. In the second panel of Figure 2.2 that point is shown as X. Production at this point ensures that utility is maximized for the economy as a whole. Note that, as in the models of comparative advantage, the opportunity cost of cloth production is given by the slope of the PPF. The slope of the PPF also yields the relative price of a unit of cloth in relation to a unit of wine (P_C/P_W). Whereas, in the models of Ricardo, differences in relative prices reflect country by country variations in labor productivities, in the standard trade model of Heckscher–Ohlin, relative price differences between countries are usually imagined to follow variations in the availability of factors of production. We take up this issue further, below.

The standard two-country, two-good, two-input trade model of Heckscher–Ohlin is typically set up with the following assumptions. First, wine and cloth differ in terms of the resources required for their production. As we noted above, wine is said to be land-intensive in its production and cloth is said to be labor-intensive. Second, our two countries A and B are imagined to vary in terms of resource availability. More specifically it is assumed that one country has greater reserves of land in relation to labor, while the other country has greater reserves of labor in relation to land. Third, within each of our two countries, the factors of production, land and labor, are mobile between each sector of production. That is, land and labor can be removed from the production of one commodity and moved into production of the other commodity. Fourth, although factors of production are mobile within countries, they are assumed to be immobile between countries. However, the final outputs, wine and cloth, can be traded between countries. Finally, once more we assume that trade costs are zero.

We make use of Figure 2.3 to explain pre-trade and post-trade differences in production and consumption within and between our two countries. The top two panels in Figure 2.3 show economic conditions in country A and country B with no trade. The bottom panels of Figure 2.3 show the post-trade patterns of production and consumption in the two countries along with the gains from trade. To follow the assumptions above, we assume that in country A land is more abundant and labor less abundant than in country B. Pre-trade production in both countries is set at the point on their respective production possibility frontiers where the two economies have both reached their highest possible indifference curves. The pre-trade relative price of cloth is shown in both countries. Notice in country A that the PPF is skewed toward wine. This reflects an assumption that country A is relatively abundant in terms of land and that the production of wine is land-intensive.

In country B, the PPF is skewed toward cloth, reflecting the labor-intensive nature of cloth production and the assumed relative abundance of labor. With no trade, country A will produce a combination of wine and cloth at point A. This is the point where country A's PPF is tangential to the highest attainable indifference curve I_1^A. The relative price of cloth (P_C^A/P_W^A) shares the slope of the PPF at point A. Note that the relative price of cloth is high when the price line is steep. At equilibrium the relative price of cloth is high in country A compared with country B, reflecting the fact that cloth is labor-intensive and that labor is relatively scarce in country A. Remember that the slope of an indifference curve is set by the opportunity cost of cloth, the amount that consumers are willing to give (pay) for cloth in terms of units of wine. Point A is thus the pre-trade **equilibrium** in panel a of Figure 2.3. At this point the slope of the indifference curve is equal to the slope of the PPF indicating that the relative price that consumers are willing to pay for cloth equals the opportunity cost of producing that cloth. With no trade, point A identifies the volume of production and consumption of our two commodities wine and cloth. At point A, we denote the amount of wine produced and consumed by Y_W^A and the amount of cloth produced and consumed by Y_C^A.

The no trade equilibrium in country B is shown by point B in panel b of Figure 2.3. This is the point where country B's PPF is tangential to the highest attainable indifference curve I_1^B. The relative price of cloth is low at this point as indicated by the slope of the price line. At point B in panel 2 the relative price that consumers are

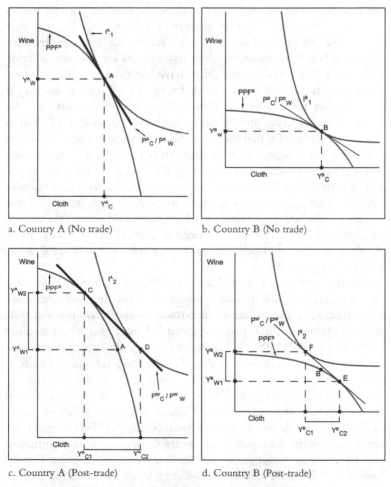

a. Country A (No trade) b. Country B (No trade)

c. Country A (Post-trade) d. Country B (Post-trade)

Figure 2.3 Gains from trade in the Heckscher–Ohlin model

willing to pay for cloth equals the opportunity cost of producing that cloth. With no trade, point B identifies the volume of production and consumption of wine and cloth when there is no trade. Y_W^B and Y_C^B represent the amount of wine and cloth consumed in country B with no trade.

Note that if the indifference curves in Figure 2.3 are all drawn with the same shape, then we are assuming that consumer demand for wine and cloth in countries A and B follows the same pattern. National variations in consumer demand are another possible reason for trade that we ignore in the presentation here.

It is the difference in domestic price ratios that forms the basis for exchange between countries when trade opens up. As soon as trade opens up and before domestic prices have had time to adjust, producers of wine in country A will see that they can sell wine in country B for a higher relative price. This will encourage exports of wine from country A to country B. At the same time, producers of cloth in country B will realize that they can export cloth to country A and sell that cloth for a higher relative price than is available domestically. Wine flows from country A to country B and cloth flows in the opposite direction. Domestic prices for wine and cloth in both countries adjust to changes in supply induced by imports and exports. Those price changes will gravitate toward a new world price that will be located somewhere between the pre-trade prices in both economies. Production of wine and cloth in the two countries will shift, following the relative price changes.

Panels c and d of Figure 2.3 show the new world relative price of cloth and the corresponding post-trade shifts in production and consumption consistent with a free-trade equilibrium. In country A, the new world relative price of cloth is lower than the pre-trade domestic price of cloth. This change in price shifts land and labor out of cloth production in country A and into wine production. In effect, country A specializes more in the production of the commodity (wine) whose relative price has increased as a result of trade. This is the commodity the production of which consumes relatively more of the abundant factor of production in country A. Following trade, production shifts from point A to point C in panel c. Consumption also moves from point A on indifference curve I_1^A to point D on a higher indifference curve I_2^A. Wine exports are illustrated in panel c as the difference $Y_{W2}^A - Y_{W1}^A$. Country A imports cloth from country

B in the amount given by $Y^A_{C2} - Y^A_{C1}$. In country B, the new world relative price of cloth is higher than the pre-trade domestic price of cloth. This change in price shifts land and labor out of wine production and into cloth production. Thus, country B specializes further in the production of cloth, the commodity whose production consumes relatively more of the abundant factor of production (labor) found in that country. Following trade, production shifts from point B to point E in panel d. Consumption also moves from point B on indifference curve I^B_1 to point F on a higher indifference curve I^B_2. Cloth exports are shown in panel d as the difference $Y^B_{C2} - Y^B_{C1}$. Country B imports wine from country A in the amount given by $Y^B_{W2} - Y^B_{W1}$. So long as the imports and exports of wine and the imports and exports of cloth are in balance, relative prices will not change at the post-trade equilibrium. Note that while countries specialize in this model as a result of trade, specialization is incomplete compared with the model of comparative advantage. This is the result of the concave shape of the PPF.

THE STOLPER–SAMUELSON THEOREM

Heckscher and Ohlin argue that the gains from trade in their model result from countries specializing in the production of commodities that use their abundant factors of production intensively. The gains from trade are seen in Figure 2.3 by the shift of country A and country B to a higher post-trade indifference curve. However, this point simply indicates that average consumption in each country is higher after trade than before trade; it says nothing about whether the benefits of trade within each country are evenly distributed across the owners of the different resources, land and labor. It turns out that the H–O model is very important to trade theorists as it also permits examination of how the gains from trade are distributed within a country.

In the example above, as trade opens, the relative prices of domestic goods produced within each country shift toward the world price. In country A, the price of wine increases relative to cloth while in country B the price of cloth increases relative to wine. These relative price changes induce shifts in production. Following the arguments of Heckscher and Ohlin, within country A resources (land and labor) are removed from cloth production and moved into wine production.

Within country B, resources are moved from wine production to cloth production. It is important to remember that wine production is land-intensive and thus increasing the volume of wine production and decreasing cloth production in country A increases the overall demand for land while reducing the overall demand for labor. Consequently, **factor prices** (input prices) adjust with the price of land (rent) rising in country A while the price of labor (wages) falls. In country B, the increase in cloth production and the decrease in wine production raise the overall demand for labor and reduce the overall demand for land such that wages rise and land rents fall. It should be clear, then, that the H–O model suggests that owners of the factor of production that is abundant within a country gain from trade while the owners of the scarce factor of production lose from trade. Thus, land-owners gain and workers lose from trade in country A, while workers gain and land-owners lose from trade in country B. It is important to note that the assumption of factor mobility within countries in the H–O model implies that owners of a factor of production face the same fate with respect to trade regardless of the sector in which their productive resource is employed. These results were first developed by the two economists Wolfgang Stolper and Paul Samuelson and are often presented as the **Stolper–Samuelson theorem**.

In later work, Paul Samuelson went on to argue that, under certain conditions, free-trade between countries also tends to equalize factor prices between countries. This **factor–price equalization theory** rests on the idea that trade effectively allows fixed factors of production to move between countries. As labor-intensive goods are exported from a low-wage country to a high-wage country, this has the effect of increasing the supply of labor in the high-wage country while reducing the effective supply of labor in the low-wage country. As a result wages in these two countries will converge. As we look at wages for specific kinds of workers we see significant variations from one country to the next. Thus, there is little general support for the factor–price equalization argument. However, trade economists can point to factor price convergence between economies with similar technologies over certain periods of time.

The H–O model's versatility allows it to be re-specified to focus on a range of interesting questions. For example, assume that two countries both use inputs of skilled labor and unskilled labor to produce computers and clothes. We assume that one country is relatively rich in terms of skilled labor and that the other country is relatively rich in terms of unskilled labor. Computer production is skilled labor-intensive and the production of clothing is unskilled labor-intensive. Combining the arguments of Heckscher and Ohlin with those of Stolper and Samuelson, we expect that trade will cause the economy that has abundant reserves of skilled labor to specialize in computer production, leaving clothes production to the country that is unskilled labor abundant. Commodity and factor prices will adjust such that the wages of skilled labor will rise and the wages of unskilled labor will fall in the country specializing in computer production. Wage inequality will rise in this country as a result of trade. In the unskilled labor-rich country producing clothes, wages of unskilled workers will increase while the wages of skilled workers will fall, causing wage levels to converge. These arguments have motivated a number of recent empirical studies that examine the impacts of import competition from less-skilled developing economies like India and China on wage inequality in advanced economies such as the United States (Autor et al., 2013; Rigby and Breau, 2008).

LEONTIEFF'S PARADOX

It is important that the theoretical models we develop show some relationship to the economic patterns that we observe in the real world. Wassily Leontieff (1953), the pioneer of input–output economics, proposed an early test of the H–O theorem. Using data on imports and exports for the US economy from 1947, Leontieff estimated the amount of capital and labor embodied within each $1 million worth of US exports and imports. Consistent with the H–O model, he expected to find the US exporting goods that were relatively capital-intensive and importing goods that were relatively labor-intensive, confirming our understanding of relative factor abundance in the United States and the rest of the world. What he discovered, however, was just the reverse: the ratio of capital to labor inputs embodied in exports from the US was lower than the capital to labor ratio embodied in imports. This result became known as **Leontieff's Paradox**.

Later tests of the claims of Heckscher and Ohlin have been a little more positive. For example, once we distinguish between skilled labor and unskilled labor, then it is possible to show that the US is a net exporter of skilled labor-intensive products and a net importer of unskilled labor-intensive products. Further, if we relax the assumption of no international differences in technology, then we also find that "effective" patterns of factor abundance can change quite significantly. To explain this, note that the productivity of one input or one factor of production can vary dramatically from one country to the next. Labor productivity tends to be considerably higher in the United States than in most other countries. This is because of investments in infrastructure (education) and technology that allow the average US worker to produce more output than her international counterparts. This means that the effective (relative) size of the labor force in the US is larger than a nominal count of US workers might suggest. Tests of the propositions of trade theory should focus on the effective size of factor inputs.

TERMS OF TRADE

The benefits of trade captured by each country depend on the **terms of trade**. The terms of trade for each country refer to the price of a country's exports relative to the price of its imports. Using the example of country A and country B in Figure 2.3, after trade country A is an exporter of wine and an importer of cloth. The terms of trade for country A are thus defined as (P_W^W/P_C^W). For country B, an exporter of cloth and importer of wine, the terms of trade are (P_C^W/P_W^W). Note from Figure 2.3 that if the world price of wine relative to the world price of cloth was higher, then the post-trade world price line (P_C^W/P_W^W) would be flatter. Country A would then move higher up its PPF and it would end up on an indifference curve higher than I_2^A. In this case the terms of trade for country A would be improving, while the terms of trade for country B would be deteriorating. If the terms of trade for a country are improving, then for each unit of exports more imports can be purchased than previously.

An important argument on the terms of trade was put forward by two economists, Hans Singer and Raul Prebisch. The **Prebisch–Singer hypothesis** states that the terms of trade for primary goods will deteriorate in relation to manufactured goods over time. The main support for this claim is that manufactured goods have a higher

income elasticity of demand than primary products. Thus, as incomes around the world increase, the demand for manufactured goods will outstrip demand for primary commodities. The Prebisch–Singer hypothesis has been used to explain the difficulties experienced by many less-developed countries as they transition through a focus on exporting primary commodities in the development process. Removing fuel and gas and other scarce resources from the list of primary commodities, there is considerable evidence in support of the Prebisch–Singer hypothesis. Over the last few decades of the twentieth century, the terms of trade for lower-priced apparel has also deteriorated, making the transition from lower technology production to higher technology production difficult for many emerging economies.

NEW TRADE THEORY: ECONOMIES OF SCALE AND IMPERFECT COMPETITION IN TRADE MODELS

The comparative advantage and H–O models of trade assume that countries engage in trade because of either differences in technology or differences in factor endowments, or sometimes both. What is important about these models is that they predict trade will take place between countries that are different from one another. However, a quick examination of international trade data, perhaps using the resources of the United Nations (Comtrade.un.org), reveals that many countries that trade with one another appear to be quite similar. Think of the trade between the United States, Germany, Japan and many other advanced industrialized nations. These countries produce many of the same sorts of commodities, with similar technologies. Indeed, the US Bureau of Economic Analysis reports that in 2014 approximately 19% of US exports flowed to countries of the European Union. In that same year, 21% of US imports originated within the European Union. The trade story becomes even messier when we see that many countries import and export what look like the same commodities. For example, in 2014 the United States exported about $146 billion of automobiles and it imported some $327 billion worth of automobiles! This is an example of intra-industry trade. It is estimated that for the United States, and many other industrialized nations, intra-industry flows of imports and exports now comprise between 60% and 70% of all trade.

In order to explain intra-industry trade we need a different set of trade models than those we have examined so far. The models of inter-industry trade considered to this point rest on two important assumptions, **perfect competition** and **constant returns to scale**. Under perfect competition we imagine that large numbers of relatively small firms are engaged in producing each type of commodity. These firms are considered price-takers: they have no influence over market prices. Constant returns to scale means that if a firm doubles all inputs to production, the firm's output will also double. In other words, altering the volume of production leaves average costs unchanged for the firm. As we shift toward explaining intra-industry trade, we abandon these assumptions in favor of **increasing returns to scale** and **monopolistic competition**. Under increasing returns to scale, doubling the inputs to production results in output gains that more than double. With increasing returns, therefore, as the scale of production expands, so average costs fall. These cost reductions are said to be internal when they are captured by a single firm, perhaps as the fixed costs of a factory building and machines are spread over more units of output. Economies of scale are said to be external when they are shared by many firms, perhaps the result of knowledge sharing that occurs when firms cluster together in space. In the discussion below, focused on monopolistic competition, the focus is on internal economies of scale. **Monopolistic competition** refers to markets where many firms compete with one another in selling different varieties of the same product. **Product differentiation** allows individual firms some control over market prices because their outputs are not perfect substitutes.

Individual firms operating within one industry produce the same commodity as one another. Under monopolistic competition it is assumed that there are many firms within an industry and that each of those firms produces a slightly different variety of the common commodity. It is also assumed that these firms experience increasing returns to scale. Without trade, increasing returns within an industry mean that the range of differentiated goods produced in that industry in a single country is smaller than the range available within the world as a whole. It is increasing returns in this environment that generates gains from trade. To see this assume that trade opens up between two countries, both of which have firms in the same sector of the economy operating under monopolistic competition.

Once again, we add the assumption of no trade costs. In the short-run with more firms in the industry (domestic and foreign), product variety increases to consumers in both countries. In turn this means that the demand for each of the product types becomes more elastic (more price sensitive). Firms will respond to the new pattern of demand by lowering their price and increasing output to capture increasing returns. Not all firms will survive the opening of domestic markets to foreign competition. However, the post-trade equilibrium will typically feature greater product variety and lower average prices than the pre-trade equilibrium. Consumers gain from the decrease in prices and from the greater variety of products offered for sale within the industry.

A somewhat different model of imperfect competition applies when the returns to scale for an individual firm are so large that international production is dominated by a very small number of firms. One example is the civilian aircraft industry, an oligopolistic market that is dominated by two firms Airbus and Boeing. In such markets global production is located in a relatively small number of countries that tend to be net exporters. The initial locations of firms in oligopolistic markets are often established through comparative advantage. Over time, scale economies get so large that they deter rival firms from entering the market even if those firms would be more efficient than existing producers if they were producing at the same scale.

With external economies of scale, markets often comprise many firms that are small in size. Expansion of such an industry in one location will lead to increases in efficiency that are shared by the firms that cluster together or **agglomerate** in space. With trade, increasing demand may lead to further economies pushing down unit prices. Unlike the standard trade model where exports lead to price increases of the exported commodity, domestic and foreign consumers can benefit from trade under external economies of scale.

NEW, NEW TRADE THEORY: GLOBAL OUTSOURCING

It has become convention to define **outsourcing** as a firm's procurement of a service or a component of a finished good from an unrelated firm. Outsourcing is said to be foreign when the two firms in question are located in different countries. Foreign outsourcing is sometimes referred to as **offshoring** when the flow of a commodity is contained within a single transnational corporation. Though we lack good data on trade in intermediate goods and services, the consensus is that there has been a remarkable increase in the practice of foreign outsourcing, the fragmentation of production activity across countries, over the last two or three decades (WTO, 2008). This increase is typically associated with sharp reductions in the costs of transportation, communications and tariffs, in short with a substantial decline in trade costs.

As we start to think about outsourcing it is important to bear in mind that the production of a large range of commodities involves the coordination of many different tasks, from research and design, to the production and assembly of various components through to advertising and sales. We often think of these tasks as forming a chain of value adding activities that transform numerous inputs through multiple stages of production into a finished commodity. In the models of trade that we have considered so far it is implicitly assumed that all such activities take place within individual firms that produce a final good from start to finish. We then look for the impacts of trade in the growth or decline of entire industries, as in the wine for cloth models of Ricardo, and in the factor markets that are closely associated with import or export sectors of the economy.

In new trade models that explore outsourcing, it is assumed that firms in different sectors of a country make decisions about what tasks of production to do themselves and which to outsource. Each task may require specific material inputs and different qualities of labor (high-skilled, semi-skilled, low-skilled). Standard arguments about comparative advantage motivate the decision to outsource production internationally so long as countries vary in terms of the relative abundance of different inputs and/or qualities of labor. Once again, the standard trade model sketched in Figure 2.3 can be used to understand the basis of trade. Instead of assuming that the X and Y axes in Figure 2.3 refer to the quantity of output of different goods, imagine they reference the volume of production of different components or services used in making a single commodity. In a common variant of this model, the different inputs are themselves assumed to be produced using varying amounts of unskilled or skilled labor. Then, countries that are relatively abundant in terms of skilled labor specialize in producing components and services the production of which is skilled labor-intensive while other countries specialize in producing inputs that are low-skilled labor-intensive. There are gains from trade in this model.

At the end of the discussion on the H–O framework above, a similar model was outlined that predicted rising wage inequality in countries that export high-skilled intensive goods and reductions in wage-inequality in countries exporting low-skilled intensive products. Unfortunately, these results are inconsistent with much empirical evidence that shows the relative wages of high-skilled workers rising around much of the world. However, newer models of outsourcing can explain these stylized facts by assuming that over time, as trade costs continue to fall, more skill-intensive components of individual commodities are outsourced from high-skilled abundant countries. Such outsourcing will increase the relative demand for high-skilled labor in the countries doing the outsourcing at the same time as more relatively high-skilled tasks are added to the economies of countries that are low-skilled labor abundant. The wages of more skilled workers in both countries will rise as a result (see Feenstra and Hanson, 2001).

It is critical to conceive of trade in these outsourcing models as focused not on finished goods but on intermediate products and services, what some have labeled individual work tasks. In these models, the impacts of trade are seen not so much in the growth and decline of individual sectors of the economy, but in terms of the performance of heterogeneous firms and workers with varying characteristics engaged in activities that are located at different stages of product value chains. Baldwin (2006) and Blinder (2006) imagine outsourcing as a new industrial revolution with the potential of globalization having a massive impact on the distribution of economic activity around the world. While Baldwin (2006) is somewhat positive about the possibilities, Blinder (2006) is decidedly not, worrying about the export of white-collar jobs as well as blue-collar jobs from developed economies such as the United States. College graduates may need to think about what types of jobs will be left for them and in what numbers.

BOX 2.1 A gravity or spatial interaction model of trade

Across the social sciences, a simple model of the interaction between two places is understood to depend upon the size of those places and the distance between them. Such models are often referred to as gravity models following the basic arguments of Newton's law of gravity that states the force of attraction between two objects is proportional to the mass of the objects and inversely proportional to the distance separating them. Within economics, Tinbergen (1962) developed a gravity model to explain the value of trade flows between countries using the gross domestic product (GDP) of each country as a measure of "mass".

According to the gravity model, trade flows between countries should rise as the value of GDP in those countries gets larger and trade flows should decline as the distance between countries increases. In simple mathematical form, we can represent this relationship as

$$TRADE_{ij} = A * (GDP_i * GDP_j * D_{ij}^{-n})$$

where TRADE is the value of trade (imports or exports) flowing between two countries i and j, GDP measures the gross domestic product in countries i and j, and D is the distance between the countries i and j. Note that the distance term has a negative exponent indicating that when distance increases the value of trade will fall. The size of the exponent, n, is not clearly specified by theory. n is a constant that is usually set at a value between 1 and 2. Higher values of this exponent imply that the friction of distance, a measure of trade cost (language barriers, institutional differences), rises more rapidly with each additional unit of distance separating the trading partners. The term A at the beginning of the gravity expression is simply a scaling constant that sets the basic relationship between the average value of trade and the average value of the gravity model.

The gravity model is relatively easy to operationalize. Let us explore a simple example using data from 2014 showing exports from the United States to its trading partners around the world. GDP data for the US and all its trading partners are used to estimate the gravity model. Distances between countries are estimated in simple Euclidean terms using the latitude and longitude marking the centroid of each country and assuming the exponent on the distance term takes a value $n = 1$.

The top panel of Figure 2.4 plots export values between the US and approximately 170 partner countries on the vertical axis. The horizontal axis plots the value of the gravity equation between the US and each of its trading partners. The overall scatterplot is positive in sign indicating that as the GDP of the US and its trading partners increase, or as the distance between the US and its trading partners falls, so predicted exports increase in value. The clustering of points around the "best-fit" line indicates that the arguments of the gravity model do a reasonable job in terms of predicting the size of actual trade flows.

The bottom panel of Figure 2.4 shows the same relationship between exports and the predicted values of trade from the gravity model relationship for Sweden and Indonesia. Sweden is a relatively small European nation, a member of the European Union. Indonesia is a relatively large emerging economy. Overall, these figures show that regardless of size and developmental status, the simple arguments of the gravity model do well in terms of predicting the level of interaction between countries.

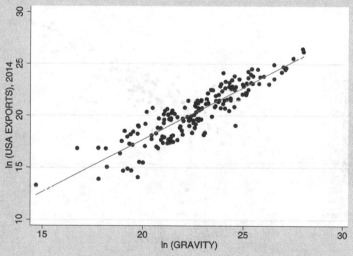

Figure 2.4 (continued)

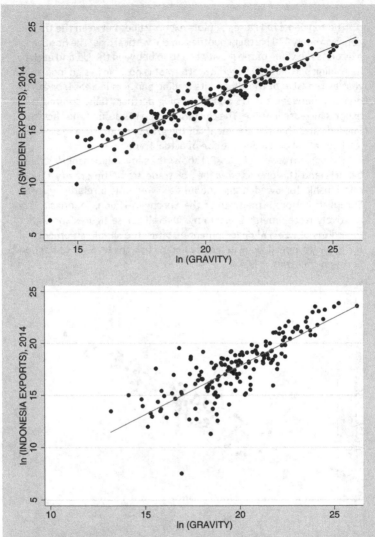

Figure 2.4 Gravity models of trade

Source: UN Comtrade provides trade data and the World Bank is the source for
GDP values.
Note: Coordinates for the centroids of each country are obtained from a
geographical information system.

SUMMARY

Trade theory has evolved significantly over time. The early one-input models of Adam Smith and David Ricardo illustrated the gains available to countries with different technologies that specialized and engaged in trade. The H–O model builds a framework for trade that focuses on factor abundance. This model has become a work-horse, of sorts, for our understanding of trade, explaining patterns of specialization and how different groups of economic agents within a country win and lose from trade. Newer trade models deploying arguments of monopolistic competition and increasing returns explain why countries that have similar factor endowments trade with one another. These arguments are developed to explain the significance of intra-industry trade that we see around much of the world. An even newer set of arguments, the so-called new, new trade theory, explores the outsourcing of intermediate goods and work tasks, often using a model of heterogeneous firms to explain the fragmentation of production within industries and its dispersion across the world economy. While the newest variants of trade theory explore offshoring activities that link different firms in different countries, in the next chapter our attention turns to transnational corporations and their separation of production activities across different countries within the firm.

The main points of this chapter are:

- The case for free trade is developed through the models of absolute advantage and comparative advantage developed by Adam Smith and David Ricardo, respectively. Comparative advantage establishes that free trade will generate gains for trading partners if each of them specializes in producing the commodity where they hold the greatest comparative advantage, the commodity where their opportunity costs are minimized.
- The H–O model explains how the gains from trade are distributed in a world with two countries, two goods and two inputs to production. The H–O model states that gains from trade will be realized when countries specialize in the production of those commodities that use their abundant factors of production intensively. Within this framework, the owners of the factor of production that is abundant within a country gain from trade

> while the owners of the scarce factor of production lose as a result of trade.
- Models of monopolistic competition explain why countries that produce the same commodities engage in trade.
- New models of global outsourcing help us understand the fragmentation of production tasks and the distribution of those tasks across countries within the global economy that are endowed with different types of factors of production.

SUGGESTED READING

A gentle introduction to comparative advantage is provided by the *Economist*. See Schools Brief: The Miracle of Trade. *The Economist*, 27 January 1996.

The World Trade Organization provides a relatively recent overview of trade theory and data. WTO (2008) *World Trade Report 2008: Trade in a Globalizing World* (available at www.wto.org/english/res_e/booksp_e/anrep_e/world_trade_report08_e.pdf)

The United Nations Conference on Trade and Development (UNCTAD) has many resources on globalization, trade and development. Check out http://unctad.org

RESOURCES

The SUNY Levin Institute has an excellent introduction to many aspects of globalization, including trade. See http://www.globalization101.org/teaching-tools/

A more orthodox account of the benefits and costs of trade is discussed at: http://www.economicsonline.co.uk/Global_economics/Why_do_countries_trade.html

Trade data may be found at UN Comtrade at: http://comtrade.un.org/

The World Bank also offers data on trade and related economic data for different countries at: http://data.worldbank.org/

The Center for International Trade at UC Davis has a wealth of trade and related data at: http://cid.econ.ucdavis.edu/

3

TRANSNATIONAL CORPORATIONS, TRADE AND THE GLOBAL ECONOMY

The world economy, measured in terms of gross domestic product (GDP), grew at an annual average rate of 2.98% between 1970 and 2014 (UNCTAD, 2015). Over this same period, world exports of goods and services expanded at an annual average rate close to 5.5%. The increase in the ratio of trade (exports) to GDP provides a simple measure of the growing integration of economic activities around the world. (However, note that the fragmentation of production between countries inflates the value of trade flows because of "double-counting", which is discussed in Box 3.2.) Between 1970 and 2014, the world **trade/GDP ratio** climbed from 10.84% to 30.1%. It is today more than three times higher than it was at the beginning of the twentieth century, an earlier period of significant international economic expansion. The global economy of the early twenty-first century is also qualitatively different from that earlier period of "arms-length" interaction, with commodity production integrated across many countries of the world in ways that we have never seen before.

Over the last few decades of the twentieth century, in what Richard Baldwin (2006) has called the "second great unbundling", commodity production tasks that were once almost fully contained within a single factory have been separated and relocated to multiple factories spread across many countries. This coordinated fragment-ation of the production process has been facilitated by far-reaching technological improvements in communications and transportation such that many goods and services in the world today are produced at different stages along complex **global value chains**. These global value or supply chains are typically managed by transnational corporations (TNCs) that move goods and services across international borders within the networks of affiliates, sub-contractors and independent suppliers that they control. It is estimated that up to 80% of all global trade is undertaken by **transnational corporations** moving inputs and outputs along their global value chains (UNCTAD, 2013a).

The aim of this chapter is to explore the rise of TNCs, to gain a better understanding of their operations and significance within the world economy, especially their role in orchestrating trade. We begin this task in the next section examining the emergence of TNCs and the reasons for their growth. We explore why firms internationalize and how TNCs organize their operations. The chapter moves ahead to show just how significant TNC activities are within the world economy, briefly presenting statistics on the growth of TNCs and foreign direct investment (FDI). The structure of the global production networks (GPNs) managed by TNCs is then discussed before analysis of the contribution of TNCs to world trade flows. A brief summary ends the chapter.

ORIGINS OF TNCS AND WHY FIRMS INTERNATIONALIZE

In the **capitalist market system** commodity production is undertaken for exchange driven by the pursuit of profit. No firm is guaranteed profit because of the vagaries of the market. A few firms attempt to manage this uncertainty by controlling markets. For most, however, competition means that they can only control the manner in which inputs are transformed into outputs, seeking advantage by increasing the efficiency of production. In this competitive environment firms are compelled to innovate, to search for new products and develop new markets, to experiment in new locations, with new sources of inputs, new processes of production and organizational routines, sure only in the knowledge that others are doing the same. It is this unending search for efficiency, driven by the uncertainty of market competition, that makes the capitalist economic system so dynamic and that generates enormous heterogeneity in the characteristics and behaviors of individual firms.

To this point, we have taken the concept of the **firm** itself as somewhat unproblematic. Since the work of Adam Smith (1776) it has been common to regard commodity production as the assembly of factors of production such as land, labor and capital (factory buildings and machinery) in order to transform materials (and services) from one form to another. As we look back in time, it is easy to imagine production as being dominated by individuals who take the materials of nature and rework them prior to consumption. Smith (1776) argued that firms exist because they are more efficient at such transformations than individual workers because of the productivity benefits associated with specialization and the division of labor. Thus we have an image of the firm as a collection of individual workers, organized by firm owners, who make use of other inputs in order to produce commodities for sale in markets. For Marx (1867) the process of commodity production under capitalism also involves the **alienation of labor**, the separation of individual workers from ownership of the means of production (the capital to control production) and thus their reliance on the market to secure wages in return for their capacity to work, their labor-power.

However, why is production organized within the firm? Why don't individuals who own different inputs used in production come together each day in the market and organize a series of temporary contracts with one another that stipulate work to be performed and payment for such work? Coase (1937) argued that firms exist because of **transaction costs**. He recognized the efficiency of the market in resource allocation, but he also noted that the search for workers and negotiations over their hiring were costly and that those costs could be reduced by coordinating open-ended employment contracts. In this model, firms are conceived as legal entities that internalize contracts for labor and other inputs rather than relying on the market.

Now that we have a clearer understanding of the existence of firms, it is important to note that the size of firms, their structure and location have changed markedly over time. In the early stages of capitalist production, most firms were relatively small, serving local markets and employing only a rudimentary division of labor. These firms engaged in mostly **artisanal** or handicraft production and because of the relatively high costs of transportation, for people and goods, they were often located close to sites of key inputs, especially labor. The development of new technologies through the industrial revolution and beyond propelled the rise of new **factory systems** of production that saw the average size of firms increase and the division of labor deepen around the use of specialized machines. Firms produced larger volumes of output for markets that were expanding, at least in part, because of innovations that reduced the costs of transport. A **spatial division of labor** emerged within many industrializing countries that was largely product-based, giving rise to the identification of cities, regions and countries with distinct sectors of the economy. The early years of the twentieth century in the core-capitalist economies saw the introduction of new assembly-line (**Fordist**) production systems that encouraged vertical integration and pushed the division of labor within firms even further. Firm location changed with new factories moving out of the city, propelling the mass-movement of workers into growing suburban neighborhoods. Competition at this time was directly tied to **economies of scale** and market-size. Mass-production requires mass-consumption and new systems of market regulation and coordination were introduced with nation-states playing a more active role in managing economies. It is important to see these shifts in the nature of production regimes within the capitalist market economy as competing experiments driven by the pursuit of profit.

The links between market size and the division of labor prompted an early internationalization of economic activity by the end of the nineteenth century. With steam-engines in ships and railways, parts of the world economy had effectively been brought closer together. To be sure, some of the connections between countries were driven by colonial bonds, but whatever their roots, the ratio of trade to GDP in the world economy as a whole accelerated sharply. It would be wrong to consider this an early phase of globalization. Though commodity trade, capital and labor flows across international borders were increasing rapidly, economic relationships remained largely what we would consider "arms-length". Most commodities were still produced from start-to-finish within one country and then sold either domestically or in international markets: there was little integration of national economies.

This began to change during the second half of the twentieth century. By the 1970s, with war-damaged economies rebuilt, competition in world markets intensified. The efficiencies of large-scale production remained but they were now deployed in at least two ways. First, new systems of **flexible accumulation** allowed volume producers to differentiate their output to meet the demands of different national regulatory regimes, consumer tastes and specialized market niches. Second, improvements in information and communications technology (ICT) dramatically reduced the costs of coordinating different stages of commodity development, manufacture and distribution, allowing the fragmentation of production activities and its distribution across many different countries. While the high costs of coordinating a sequence of production tasks once tied these activities to one another in a specific location, this is no longer the case. The separation of production activities that utilize different inputs is encouraged by significant geographical differences in factor abundance and cost, in market structure and in the knowledge production capabilities of economic agents in various locations. A new spatial division of labor has emerged that is less dependent upon products as it is upon skills and the availability of different kinds of knowledge in different places.

Control of production still largely resides within individual firms. However, firms now find themselves variously caught up in complex webs of interactions that bond them to one another and to places in ways that make it extremely difficult to identify the boundaries of individual corporations and national economies. For Peter Dicken (2015), the engines of the global economy are the TNCs that spin these webs. The TNC is defined as a firm/corporate entity that owns or controls value adding activities in more than one country. Figure 3.1 provides an example of a TNC, illustrating the global reach of Toyota's production operations. With fifty-four overseas manufacturing subsidiaries distributed across twenty-eight countries, in 2014 Toyota Motor Corporation was the second largest automobile company in the world by volume, producing more than 10 million vehicles sold in approximately 170 countries. More than 60% of Toyota's total assets, 64% of its sales and about 38% of its worldwide workforce are located outside Japan, giving Toyota a transnationality index value of 55% in 2013.

The **transnationality index** provides a simple measure of the extent to which a TNC's activities are distributed outside the country where its headquarters are located. The index value is calculated as the average of three ratios—the ratio of foreign assets to total assets,

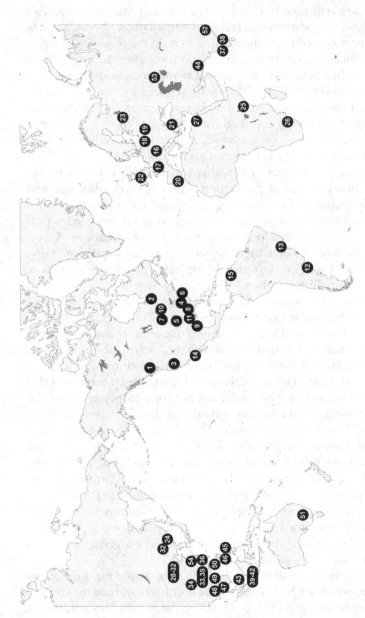

Figure 3.1 Toyota's global production network

Source: http://www.toyota-global.com

Note: The nodes represent the location of Toyota overseas manufacturing plants around the world.

the ratio of foreign sales to total sales and the ratio of foreign employment to total employment.

Why do firms organize their activities across more than one national economy; why do they establish subsidiaries and partnerships in countries other than those in which they originate? Orthodox economics has been relatively silent on this question, at least in part because standard models of perfect competition do not provide much room for individual firms to generate the capabilities that would allow them to compete in foreign markets complicated by different cultural, political and legal systems. In 1976 Stephen Hymer rejected the assumptions of perfect competition in proposing arguments from the field of industrial organization to explain that firms could compete in foreign markets if they possessed **ownership-specific advantages** that would offset the cost and risk of operating in more than one country. These advantages might be related to size (large firms can generate economies of scale and scope), to specific technological advantages, to managerial skills, to superior marketing capabilities and so on. Dunning (1979) extended Hymer's arguments in his "eclectic paradigm" or model of international production. The first part of this model rests on the ownership advantage arguments of Hymer. To these claims Dunning adds transactions cost economics, encountered above, to examine the conditions under which it makes sense for firms to internalize their advantages rather than trade them in the market (perhaps in the form of licensing other firms to produce and/or sell their output). Finally, he proposes that there must be location-specific factors that make it more profitable for the firm to exploit its internalized advantages in a foreign location rather than simply exporting goods to foreign markets. For Dunning, then, a firm will become a TNC when it generates ownership-specific advantages, when it chooses to internalize these advantages and when it decides to pursue its advantages in a foreign location.

The broader literature identifies two primary drivers for the transnational organization of production, access to foreign markets and access to foreign assets (Dicken, 2015). However, we must add to these factors a range of strategic considerations that make a foreign presence attractive. In terms of market access, it is important to note that the geography of the world economy has altered more dramatically over the last fifty years than in the previous few hundred years. These changes have resulted from geographical variations in population dynamics, from independence and secession, from the rapid growth of a number of less-developed countries and from the transition of state-controlled economies to market forms of governance. It is certainly possible that expanding foreign markets could be served by exports alone, but the existence of tariff and non-tariff trade barriers (see Chapter 4) provides strong incentives to internationalize.

Strategy in uncertain, often rapidly changing, markets provides another incentive for TNCs to emerge. Volkswagen adopted an early international position as a hedge against currency fluctuations and a Deutsche Mark that was rapidly increasing in relative value. Apple, Microsoft, General Electric and many other US based TNCs established overseas subsidiaries in which to park global revenues and avoid relatively high corporate tax rates in the United States. Isolating legal liabilities within particular nation-states is another reason for TNC expansion. In 1984, a toxic chemical cloud was accidentally generated by US owned Union Carbide at its plant in Bhopal, India. Three thousand people died. The Indian government filed a legal suit against Union Carbide but no representatives of the company have ever been charged. Attempts to seek compensation within US courts proved unsuccessful. The Indian government finally reached a settlement with Union Carbide, though continuing litigation led to the dismantling of Union Carbide India Ltd as the parent company sought to limit further damage claims.

Table 3.1 lists the top twenty non-financial TNCs in terms of foreign assets in 2012–13. A brief glance at this table should provide a clear understanding of how the search for inputs to the production process drives the global spread of TNCs at least in some sectors of the economy. Of the ten corporations listed in Table 3.1, five are in the petroleum and gas industry. For these TNCs, and others across natural resource industries, access to scarce raw material sites is critical. Most other TNCs rely heavily on different kinds of inputs to production such as skilled or unskilled labor, knowledge, cheap energy or even lax environmental and labor legislation, all of which are distributed unevenly around the world.

TNCs often form to exploit geographies of factor abundance and thus the varying prices that must be paid to secure key inputs to production around the global economy. This exploitation often takes the form of moving segments of their operations to locations where they can be most efficiently developed. As noted above, this

Table 3.1 Top twenty non-financial TNCs, 2012–13

Company	Country of origin	Industry	TNI index
General Electric Co.	United States	Electrical & electronic equipment	52.5
Royal Dutch Shell plc	United Kingdom	Petroleum expl./ref./distr.	76.6
BP plc	United Kingdom	Petroleum expl./ref./distr.	83.8
Toyota Motor Corporation	Japan	Motor vehicles	54.7
Total SA	France	Petroleum expl./ref./distr.	78.5
Exxon Mobil Corporation	United States	Petroleum expl./ref./distr.	65.4
Vodafone Group Plc	United Kingdom	Telecommunications	90.4
GDF Suez	France	Utilities (electricity, gas and water)	59.2
Chevron Corporation	United States	Petroleum expl./ref./distr.	59.5
Volkswagen Group	Germany	Motor vehicles	58.2
Eni SpA	Italy	Petroleum expl./ref./distr.	63.3
Nestlé SA	Switzerland	Food, beverages and tobacco	97.1
Enel SpA	Italy	Electricity, gas and water	56.6
E.ON AG	Germany	Utilities (electricity, gas and water)	65.0
Anheuser-Busch InBev NV	Belgium	Food, beverages and tobacco	92.8
ArcelorMittal	Luxembourg	Metal and metal products	91.1
Siemens AG	Germany	Electrical & electronic equipment	77.9
Honda Motor Co. Ltd	Japan	Motor vehicles	73.4
Mitsubishi Corporation	Japan	Wholesale trade	40.6
EDF SA	France	Utilities (electricity, gas and water)	30.8

Source: UNCTAD, 2013a.

Note: expl.—exploration; ref.—refining; distr.—distribution

fragmentation of production stages only makes sense when the division of labor is relatively deep and when the costs of transportation and communications are sufficiently low as not to eliminate the cost-savings of a global position.

Just as many individual corporations have assumed a transnational footprint, so a number of countries around the world have economies that depend heavily on the activities of TNCs. Developing economies, in particular, look to TNCs as sources of capital investment, job creation and technological diffusion. Advanced industrialized countries, too, play host to TNCs from other developed economies and increasingly to TNCs originating in emerging economies. Countries themselves have "gone global", some in the form of overseas investments through sovereign wealth funds (state-owned investment funds), diversifying their portfolios outside their national territories. All these flows raise questions about who controls economic activity within particular territorial units and what "external" control might mean for the future. In Box 3.1, the "foreign ownership/control" of Singapore's economy is examined.

BOX 3.1 Ownership and control of Singapore's economy

Singapore is a relatively small city-state located at the bottom of the Malay archipelago. Long a colony of the British Empire, the country was officially created with independence from Malaysia in 1965. Despite a favorable geographic location with a protected harbor at the mouth of the Malacca Strait, through which approximately one-third of world maritime trade transits, Singapore's economic growth was very much in doubt when Lee Kuan Yew became the country's first prime minister. Lee established a stable, authoritarian government that carefully directed economic expansion financed largely by foreign capital in the form of foreign direct investment (FDI). With a population of about 5.5 million and a gross domestic product (GDP) of approximately US$308 billion, in 2014 Singapore ranked in the top ten of all countries in the world in terms of GDP per capita.

Singapore remains one of the most open or "globalized" economies in the world with a trade (imports + exports) to GDP ratio of around 2.5 (for the world as a whole this ratio was just under 0.6 in 2013, according to the World Trade Organization). Singapore still relies heavily on foreign capital to fund investment in its economy, ranking sixth in the world as a host economy in terms of FDI (UNCTAD, 2015). Much of the production that occurs within Singapore is related to the activities of TNC directed global value chains (GVCs). UNCTAD estimates that 82% of the country's exports are dependent upon GVCs, a higher share than in any other of the other top twenty-five exporting nations in the world (UNCTAD, 2013a). The prominent role of TNCs within Singapore's economy raises important questions about economic ownership and control within that nation. Does Singapore's reliance on global capital inflows, on TNCs and foreign markets, make it vulnerable within the global economy, or does the transnational character of Singapore's economy provide a measure of resilience in a multi-polar world?

THE GROWTH OF TRANSNATIONAL CORPORATIONS

The emergence of the global economy proceeded hand-in-hand with the growth in the number and the significance of TNCs. That growth was relatively fitful at first. Today's TNCs might be traced back to the holdings of international financial institutions such as the Medici Bank operating across Europe in the fifteenth century, to the guilds of merchant capitalists like the Hansa, uniting and protecting Baltic and north European traders from the fourteenth to the seventeenth centuries, and to the state–sponsored trading companies that appeared in the late sixteenth and the seventeenth centuries. The (English) East India Company, the Dutch East India Company and the Hudson's Bay Company were prominent examples of the latter, engaged largely in forms of arbitrage involving exotic foods, spices, furs and other raw materials. The Royal Africa Company was better known for its focus on the slave-trade linking England, West Africa and the Americas.

It was not really until the mid-nineteenth century that the TNC, as defined above, made its appearance upon the economic landscape. Indeed, Wilkins (2001) notes that "Only with steamships, railroads and cables" was the effective management of TNCs possible. To these technologies we can add changes in the nature of limited liability law, growth in international banking and equity markets that limited risk and assisted firms in crossing international borders. Much of the early growth of TNCs was associated with securing supplies of primary materials. In the United States, the growth of Standard Oil (see Chapter 1) and the United Fruit Company are prominent examples. The United Fruit Company, established late in the eighteenth century, monopolized banana production across much of Central America, developing a neocolonial plantation system, along with railroads and ports to ship its produce. Strong links to host-governments, the so-called "banana republics", assured the growth of United Fruit, though its political entanglements also sowed the seeds of the company's eventual demise. The Royal Dutch Petroleum Corporation, later to become Royal Dutch Shell, was founded in 1890 to develop Sumatran oil-fields, driven in part by competition with Standard Oil to secure petroleum reserves throughout different parts of the world. Rio Tinto in mining, Dunlop in rubber production and Cadbury in cocoa and chocolate production are other prominent examples of early resource-based TNCs.

The first manufacturing TNCs emerged in the latter part of the nineteenth century. In 1855, the German electrical equipment corporation Siemens opened an assembly plant in St. Petersburg, Russia focused on telegraph equipment, and a British subsidiary opened shortly thereafter. Merck, the German pharmaceuticals firm, established production operations in the United States following significant increases in tariffs. The US firm Singer Manufacturing Company, maker of sewing machines, built a dedicated manufacturing facility in Scotland in 1867 to meet the demands of the British market for its products. Factories in Canada, Germany and Russia soon followed. In similar fashion, Eastman Kodak expanded manufacturing operations into the UK when its exports failed to keep up with growing European demand (Cohen, 2007).

Two World Wars and the Great Depression slowed TNC expansion in the first half of the twentieth century. However, postwar redevelopment, a raft of new technologies and sustained growth in average incomes, at least in the advanced industrialized economies, stimulated rapid growth in the number of TNCs operating in the world economy. Figure 3.2 provides a general overview of growth in the number of TNCs operating in the world economy and in accumulated stocks of **foreign direct investment** since 1950. Global GDP data are shown as a reference to indicate just how significant has been the recent growth in TNCs and related direct investment. FDI is defined as an investment that crosses an international

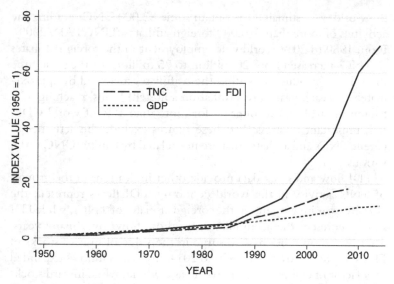

Figure 3.2 Growth of TNCs and FDI

Sources: UNCTAD, various years; Maddison-Project, 2013 (http://www.ggdc.net/maddison/maddison-project/home.htm)

border for the purpose of owning or controlling value adding activity in another country. Direct investment is typically distinguished from portfolio investment, the latter undertaken without any expectation of controlling production operations. It is difficult to generate reliable data on the activities of TNCs, and FDI is often used as a proxy measure, a surrogate, of TNC activity. Capital flows between countries, as part of national accounts and balance of payments data, have been tracked for more than a century.

Between 1870 and 1970 the number of TNCs operating in the world economy increased by a factor of three to a little more than 7,300. Over the next twenty years TNC activity exploded around the world. UNCTAD estimates that by 1990 approximately 37,000 parent TNCs controlled close to 170,000 affiliates in a rapidly globalizing world economy. An affiliate is a foreign firm in which a parent TNC has at least a 10% equity stake. TNCs often control related firms through various forms of non-equity arrangements, such as sub-contracting, and thus estimates of TNC operations are generally regarded as undercounts of their overall impact. By 2008, the world was estimated to contain some 82,000 TNCs guiding the activities of more than 810,000 foreign affiliates (UNCTAD, 2009). From 1980 to 2014 worldwide employment in the foreign affiliates of TNCs increased from 20 million to 75 million. At the same time the value of production within these affiliates increased by approximately 7% each year in real (inflation adjusted) terms, reaching $7.9 trillion in 2014 and accounting for more than 10% of world GDP. It is important to stress that these figures exclude the activities of parent TNCs and affiliates that are not related by equity (UNCTAD, various years).

FDI flow and stock data provide other indications of the growth of TNC activity in the world economy. FDI flows represent the year-by-year investments in the foreign affiliates of TNCs, while FDI stocks represent the accumulation of those flows over many years. Table 3.2 shows the massive surge in the value of inward stocks of FDI after the 1970s. From 1970 to 2014, inward FDI flows expanded by a factor of eighteen for the world as a whole, while inward stocks of FDI expanded by a factor of fourteen since 1980. FDI data are available annually through UNCTAD from 1970; earlier estimates derive from a variety of sources (Cohen, 2007). Investments tend to be highly volatile and so FDI inward and outward flows show sharp swings from one year to the next reflecting investor expectations about changing economic fortunes across firms, sectors and national economies. Stock data smooth these annual fluctuations to a significant degree. Inward FDI, the flows and stocks of direct investment entering an economy from the rest of the world, is often a little different in value from the outward flows of FDI leaving an economy. The inward data are generally considered more accurate than the outward flows.

Across the twentieth century, the countries of origin and the destinations of FDI have changed considerably. At the start of the century, the UK was the source of close to 50% of the world's FDI with the United States, the second most important source nation, controlling a little more than 15% of outward FDI. Germany, France and the Netherlands were the next leading source nations. The positions of the UK and the US were reversed after the Second World War. In the 1960s, following the establishment of the European Common Market, the forerunner of today's European Union (see Chapter 4), US transnational manufacturing firms began setting up production operations in Europe, concerned about the possibility of losing market access. By the early 1970s, six times as much FDI was flowing out of the US each year than flowing in, giving rise to the popular expression that globalization was the Americanization of the world economy. In the early 1980s, the US was responsible for approximately 40% of the world's FDI, that share declining to about 25% by 2000, roughly where it stands today. The European share of the world's outward FDI flow has fluctuated between 25% and 31% since 2010. Perhaps the most remarkable recent shift in terms of the geographical origins of FDI flows has been the rise of the developing economies. As late as 2000 less than 10% of FDI outflows originated in the developing world. By 2014 this share had more than tripled to 35%, about half these flows coming from China, including Hong Kong, alone.

In the early years of the twentieth century, Latin America was the largest recipient of the world's FDI, capturing about one-third of all such inflows. Asian nations as a whole absorbed a little more than 20% of the world's inward FDI, and Western Europe and the United States both received about 10% of FDI inflows. Many of these flows, particularly those directed toward Latin America and Asia, were focused on primary resource acquisition as discussed above. From 1960 to the early 1980s, much of the growth of inward FDI flows was directed at market access and thus captured by developed market economies. FDI flows to the US increased steadily but remained only about half the value of such flows that ended up in Europe. FDI inflows to Latin America, Asia and Africa declined sharply at this time. By the end of the twentieth century, Europe was still the favored destination of FDI, soaking up perhaps 35% of all such flows, though the United States remained the country with the largest inflows of FDI. Selected Asian nations rebounded as destinations for FDI by the early 1990s as industrialized countries increasingly sought access to lower-cost sites of assembly for manufactured products. Into the early years of the twenty-first century, the attraction of TNCs and FDI flows became a more important component of the development strategies of most lower-income economies from Asia to Africa and through Latin America. More and more of this FDI was driven by the offshoring of manufacturing and service sector jobs from the industrialized world. By 2014 these flows had become so large that developing countries absorbed more than 55%

of the world's inward FDI, and China and Hong Kong both received more FDI inflows than the United States. The FDI push into developing economies witnessed even more changes in the first half of 2105 as India overtook China as the leading recipient country of inward FDI.

Table 3.2 provides a smoothed representation of the origins and destinations of FDI flows, reporting accumulated stocks of FDI inflows and outflows for selected countries and regions since 1980. The values in this table correspond broadly to the discussion above, though note that the flow data change more rapidly from one period to the next. For example, the accumulated stocks of outward FDI for the European Union stand at more than 40% in 2010 compared to the 2010 FDI outflow share of 31%. Further, as the recent flow of outward FDI from the developing world accelerates, it will take a number of years for the accumulated stock of such investment to catch up to the flow share.

TNC activity has traditionally focused on specific sectors of the economy. Throughout much of the first half of the twentieth century

Table 3.2 Shares of world inward and outward FDI stocks (%)

	Inward stock				Outward stock			
	1980	1990	2000	2010	1980	1990	2000	2010
Developed countries	75.6	74.0	68.5	65.3	96.9	95.3	87.8	82.3
EU	42.5	39.2	37.6	36.0	40.7	45.2	47.1	43.8
Japan	0.7	0.6	0.6	1.1	3.7	11.7	4.7	4.1
US	16.8	22.1	21.7	18.0	42.0	25.1	20.8	23.7
Developing countries	24.4	25.8	30.3	31.1	3.1	4.6	11.9	15.3
Africa	3.9	2.1	2.6	2.9	0.2	0.7	0.3	0.6
LAC	8.9	6.2	9.3	9.0	1.7	1.1	1.9	3.6
Asia & Pac.	11.7	17.5	18.4	19.2	1.2	2.8	9.7	11.1
C&E Europe		0.2	1.2	3.6		0.1	0.3	2.4

Source: UNCTAD, various years

Notes: The values are percentages. EU is European Union, LAC is Latin America and Caribbean, C&E Europe is Central and Eastern Europe, and Asia & Pac. includes Asia and Pacific nations. Note that these shares vary quite dramatically across different years of the UNCTAD World Investment Reports.

FDI was largely directed toward primary resources, securing access to oil and gas, to ores and mineral inputs for manufacturing, and to agricultural goods. During the second half of the twentieth century, FDI was much more heavily concentrated on manufacturing activity and since 1990 on services. Separating FDI stocks into shares across primary, secondary (manufacturing) and tertiary (service) sectors yields the following distributions: 1975 (24%, 42%, 34%), 1990 (12%, 40%, 48%), 2000 (8%, 35%, 57%), 2012 (10%, 27%, 63%). The growth of service sector FDI reflects a similar reorientation of employment and GDP to services production and delivery over the last few decades, driven originally by investment in finance and insurance and more recently by investment flows into information and communications technologies, utilities (oil, gas and electrical provision) and retailing. It is important to note that the growth of service sector FDI has been just as marked within the developing countries of the world as it has within the developed economies.

GLOBAL PRODUCTION NETWORKS AND COMMODITY VALUE CHAINS

How do TNCs organize their activities within a dynamic global economy? It is important for us to consider this question because the way in which TNCs structure their business operations and their relationships with foreign affiliates, with firms that are unrelated in terms of equity and with other economic agents and institutions has an important influence on trade, on the flow of goods and services, between regions of the global economy. (Of course, firms that are not TNCs buy and sell goods outside the countries where they are located and thus also contribute to trade.) Although relatively few in number, compared with business establishments overall, TNCs display considerable variety in terms of structure and organization, those characteristics reflecting the nature of the economic sectors in which they are found (the physical requirements of commodity production and consumer expectations), the locations in which they operate (the institutional and regulatory structures of cities, regions and nations) and the business cultures of the places where they originate. Though the Japanese management consultant and hyper-globalist Keniche Ohmae (1990) celebrates a borderless global economy controlled by placeless TNCs, Doremus et al. (1998) seek to shatter the myth of the global corporation, noting that the places where firms (TNCs) develop leave enduring imprints on their subsequent behavior. Dicken (2015) provides a glimpse of the distinctive characteristics of the Japanese keiretsu, intercorporate alliances that bind diversified firms to one another across sectors of the economy, the family-owned, vertically integrated production networks of the Korean chaebol, and how these differ from the structure of overseas Chinese business networks and patterns of industrial organization that are more common in Europe and in the United States.

Much of the research that examines the structure of the emerging global economy, the links between TNCs and other firms, between state and non-state institutions that regulate markets, and between the places where production and consumption occur and where lives are constructed make use of the concept of the **commodity value chain**. For Sturgeon (2001), following Gereffi and Korzeneiwicz (1994), the commodity value chain identifies a sequence of activities involved in moving a particular product, a service or more tangible commodity, from conception to market and beyond. In Figure 3.3 the critical steps in the commodity value chain are identified,

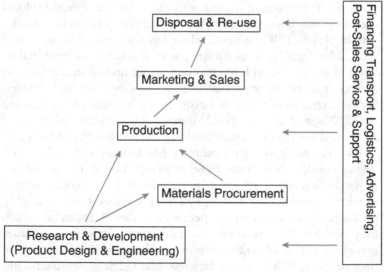

Figure 3.3 The global commodity chain
Source: Gereffi et al. (2005)

beginning with research and development, through resource provisioning, to production, distribution and sale. These chains may be extended by exploring the life cycles of products, waste and recycling, and they recognize that many related activities such as finance, transportation, logistics, marketing and post-sales service are necessary for the chain to operate. When these commodity chains incorporate an international dimension, then we use the concept of the **global commodity chain** (GCC). Of most interest in the GCC literature is where the different steps in the chain are located, what firms are engaged in the different tasks along the chain, and how the chain is governed.

A closely related concept to the GCC is the **global production network**. The GPN is also focused on the organization, the geography and the coordination of value adding activities (Coe et al., 2004). For Coe and Yeung (2015), the GPN overcomes the linearity of the commodity chain model and better reflects the multiplicity of connections between firm and non-firm actors within and across territories and different commodity production systems. Supporters of the GPN framework also claim that it makes clearer the dynamism of global production arrangements that are continuously being redrawn as firms and other political-economic agents contest distributions of economic and political power. For us, the GPN is most readily understood as the constellation of firms and other economic agents, states and non-state institutions operating across various spatial scales that influence the creation and the distribution of economic value. As TNCs increasingly play the lead role in coordinating and controlling these global networks and resulting trade flows, so we shift to examine how TNCs organize and coordinate the GCCs or production networks within which they are embedded to a greater or lesser extent.

Production networks tie together a number of firms, large and small, some domestic and some transnational in their operations. These firms are linked in different ways to one or a number of their network partners depending on how the activities along commodity chains are fragmented. This fragmentation, in turn, is shaped by product and process technologies, by geographical variations in production costs, by logistical and institutional considerations and by the forces of competition that drive continual adjustment across all these parameters. The operation of GPNs is strongly influenced by the different kinds of TNCs that tend to dominate their organization and coordination. These TNCs have to choose which functions along a commodity chain to perform internally, which functions should be outsourced to other firms, what forms outsourcing should take and how external partners should be managed, and where the different value adding components of the production network should be located.

It is important to distinguish between two different sorts of transactions that TNCs engage in as they operate within production networks. Those transactions that take place within the boundaries of the TNC we designate as **internal transactions** and those that cross the boundaries of the TNC and involve exchanges between the TNC and other firms in which the TNC has no equity position we designate as **external transactions**. (The growing significance of non-equity forms of TNC related activities are explored by UNCTAD (2011a) in the *World Investment Report* of 2011.) Internal transactions are not closely mediated by the market; rather they are controlled by the corporate headquarters of the TNC and structured to achieve various goals such as lowering production costs, acquiring and protecting TNC-specific knowledge or limiting profits that are exposed to higher rates of taxation. One way of thinking about internal transactions is to focus on the relationships and the flows that tie together the individual establishments that comprise the TNC. While this might sound straightforward, it is complicated by the fact that the boundaries of the TNC are sometimes difficult to establish. While it is clear that wholly owned subsidiaries, foreign or domestic, are part of a single TNC, it is less clear how to position affiliated firms in which one or more TNCs might hold a partial equity stake. Historically, the core functions of the TNC, such as developing firm strategy, financial decision-making and research and development, were performed within or close to the corporate headquarters of the TNC, while production and marketing operations were distributed across a number of countries. However, as international markets are increasingly differentiated and as new sites of knowledge production emerge within many industrial sectors, so TNCs rely more and more on their wholly owned subsidiaries and affiliates located in different countries to gather market intelligence and extend their technological competence. In these ways, the core functions of the TNC themselves are becoming more geographically differentiated.

The external transactions of TNCs may take a number of different forms including relatively ephemeral arms-length exchanges with multiple parties, to more stable **outsourcing** relationships with **subcontracting partners**, through to **strategic alliances** and **joint ventures**. When the transactions between a TNC and unrelated firms are ephemeral we consider such transactions as governed largely by the dictates of the competitive marketplace. Such transactions typically involve commodities that are highly standardized. If the TNC requires more regular flows of inputs with specific qualities it will typically seek an external partner to supply those inputs. This process whereby individual firms, including TNCs, outsource some or all of the tasks that are required to produce a particular commodity, a good or a service, is known as subcontracting. Some firms outsource all of the tasks involved in producing a finished good and then sell that good under their own brand name. This is very common in the household appliance industry and in the clothing sector. Common examples of firms that rely on large networks of subcontractors are Dell and Nike. In other cases firms outsource only some production stages perhaps seeking to maintain internal control over more critical or sensitive tasks. Inter-firm networks are also produced through strategic alliances and joint-ventures. Strategic alliances are formed when individual firms decide to share subsets of their assets (unlike in mergers and acquisitions where firm assets are completely shared) to achieve a specific goal. This is common when pooling assets makes sense but when individual firms seek to maintain their overall identity. One example is the airline industry where individual airlines have formed alliances to code-share and thus sell more flights as their own, to share some ground-handling, maintenance, check-in and marketing costs. Joint ventures are undertaken for many of the same reasons as strategic alliances, to combine the strengths of individual firms and share the costs of developing risky technologies or to explore new markets. Unlike strategic alliances, joint ventures result in the formation of a new corporate entity from the assets of the partners involved. The streaming website Hulu is a well-known joint venture that was launched by the US television corporations NBC, Fox and Disney-ABC.

Resource-based views of the firm (Barney, 1991) argue that individual economic agents have different sets of competencies that limit the types of economic activities in which they can profitably create value. Few, if any, firms, TNCs included, have broad enough sets of capabilities to allow them to efficiently internalize entire commodity chains. A simple model of the decision of TNCs to internalize parts of GCCs and to outsource other parts rests on the same transaction-cost arguments reviewed earlier in this chapter. Gereffi et al. (2005) argue that TNCs are more likely to outsource functions that involve the production of standardized products because inter-firm contracts for such functions are relatively simple to write and because the market efficiently regulates such contracts given the large number of firms that have the capability of producing the products involved. More customized products and services are typically more technically demanding and the outsourcing of such activities involves higher levels of transaction-specific investment and thus greater risks of opportunism. For these reasons, such activities are more likely to be performed internally by the TNC or through the use of long-run strategic partners. Building on these arguments, Gereffi et al. (2005) identify five different forms of GPNs and their coordination that span different mixes of intra-firm and inter-firm transactions (see Figure 3.4). These forms are distinguished on the basis of the complexity of the transactions involved, the extent to which technological requirements and transactional demands can be codified, and the capabilities of suppliers. At opposite ends of their model of production network governance sit the market and the vertically integrated firm. Three additional types of network governance form the core of their framework, and are highlighted in Table 3.3.

CAPTURING VALUE IN GLOBAL PRODUCTION NETWORKS

In Chapter 5 we explore some of the linkages between international trade and development. As a brief precursor to that discussion it is important to note the role that TNCs play in spreading investment, employment and economic growth across different parts of the global economy. By engaging in FDI or by sourcing inputs from independent foreign firms, TNCs spread capital investment and jobs across international borders. In developing countries, where incomes are relatively low and the potential for raising domestic capital limited, these flows can play an important role in terms of capital formation.

Form of network governance	Complexity of transactions	Ability to codify transactions	Capabilities of suppliers	Index of coordination & power asymmetry
Hierarchy Vertically integrated firms, close control of inputs & outputs	High	Low	Low	HIGH
Captive Suppliers with limited capabilities closely governed by lead firms encourage transactional dependence	High	High	Low	
Relational Complex transactions with skilled suppliers lead to mutual dependence	High	Low	High	
Modular Technical standards codify knowledge & sophisticated suppliers can supply complete products or modules if architecture is discrete	High	High	High	
Market Transactions codified & simple, switching costs low for buyers & sellers	Low	High	High	LOW

Figure 3.4 Different forms of global production networks and governance

Source: Gereffi et al. (2005)

The possibility of knowledge transfers across firms within value chains and the absorption of that knowledge in the firms and workers of host economies also raise prospects for longer-run growth.

Whether or not these prospects are realized depends on many factors including which parts of value chains get located within different countries and how well host economies are able to integrate and leverage value chain resources to the rest of their economies. While the power of TNCs ensures that they retain control over the distribution of value adding activities, the geographical distribution of those activities has perhaps never been less certain. In this respect the role of nation-state policy is critical in terms of building long-run production capabilities and growth futures. From education to capital- and labor-market regulation, through to trade policy, nation-states shape institutional structures that influence how countries engage in GPNs and whether that engagement is a net positive for different groups in society. Some of the impacts of this engagement are discussed further in Chapter 6.

TNCS AND TRADE

To this point in the chapter we have discussed the emergence and growth of TNCs within the global economy. Our interest in TNCs in this book on trade reflects the fact that because TNCs control economic activity in more than one country their operations exert a strong influence on the volume and direction of trade flows around much of the world. How strong is this influence? In 2010 total world exports of goods and services were valued at approximately $19 trillion. Of this figure, some $6.3 trillion of exports flowed between TNCs and their worldwide affiliates (internal transactions) and a further $8.7 trillion of global exports were directed by TNC activities involving arms-length trade or trade with non-equity partners (external transactions) (UNCTAD, 2013a). Thus, it is estimated that approximately 80% of all world trade (in the form of gross exports) is related to the GPNs controlled by TNCs.

Within different sectors of the economy and within different countries the role of TNCs in directing trade varies. In the natural resource processing sectors, TNCs dominate global production and trade, at least in part, because of the high costs of exploration. Within manufacturing, TNC related trade is greater in industries where production tasks are more readily separated such as automobile production and electronics. And, there is broad agreement of the rising importance of global TNCs in services trade. Turning to geography, the Survey of Current Business reports that US MNCs comprise approximately 48% of the nation's exports and 42% of its imports. Adding the activities of foreign MNCs in the US to these figures suggests that approximately two-thirds of US imports and exports are directed by global TNCs (Barefoot, 2012). UNCTAD estimates similar levels of TNC driven trade for France, higher levels for China, and that more than 90% of Japanese exports of goods and services can be linked to TNC activity.

BOX 3.2   Double-counting and value added trade measures

The production of all goods and services in the economy involves the consumption of inputs of various sorts. Inputs of energy, raw materials and labor are clearly recognized as critical to most production activity. Inputs of intermediate or semi-finished goods are increasingly important to consider when commodity production is increasingly fragmented across firms located in different places. Individual firms produce output that, in most cases, has a value greater than the value of the inputs that they consume. Indeed, if this was not generally the case, economic activity would make little sense. The difference between the value of a firm's output (revenue) and its purchase of energy and materials (including intermediate inputs) is known as value added. While the gross output of the firm may be equated with its revenue, the net output of the firm is equivalent to its value added. If we sum the value added across all firms operating within a country over a unit period of time, say a year, then the result is the country's value added, the new value that economic activity within the country has added in the year. This sum is conventionally defined as the country's gross domestic product (GDP).

Let us assume for the moment that firms produce their output within one country and that they purchase all the inputs required for production within that same country. If these firms can only sell their output within the country in which they are located, there are no exports and a country's GDP is limited by the size of the national market. With exports a country can increase its overall sales and thus raise domestic GDP. In this simple model, exporting adds jobs and it increases the net wealth produced by the country that exports.

If we relax these assumptions and we allow firms (TNCs) to produce commodities in different stages in more than one country, then the simple relationships between a country's gross exports, GDP and value added are broken. To see this, consider the following example.

In Table 3.3 there are four stages to the value chain of a commodity from raw material extraction, through two stages of processing, to final consumption. Each of these stages is located in a different country. We ignore the costs of energy and materials that are consumed in each country as part of the production process and focus only on the value added created in each country. We assume that firms in country 1 extract raw materials and export them to country 2. Let us assume that 5 units of value added are created in this process. Thus country 1 offers for sale goods valued at 5 units and these goods are exported to country 2. In country 2 the raw materials undergo processing. Assume that this stage of commodity transformation adds 5 more units of value added. The total value of goods offered for sale in country 2 is 10 units. Note that 5 units of this value derive from production activities in country 1. Country 2 exports its output to country 3 for further processing in a manufacturing stage. We assume, once more, that this next stage of processing adds 5 more units of value added to the gross value of the goods offered for sale. Country 3 thus offers for sale goods valued at 15 units that are exported to country 4 for final consumption. The total value of gross exports in this world equals 30 units. However, only 15 units of value added were created in Table 3.3. Thus, 50% of the value of gross exports results from double-counting the value added of countries 1 and 2.

This may seem like a trivial example; however, it captures the reality of world trade data that are based on gross rather than net flows. Thus, examining imports and exports alone makes it difficult to understand the role of individual countries in the global production networks that characterize the world economy today. The double-counting problem just outlined gets worse as the length of global value chains, the number of times semi-finished goods are shipped across international borders, increases. Using new databases (UNCTAD-Eora, OECD/WTO and IDE-JETRO) that track value added trade, it is becoming possible to calculate the extent to which different industries and countries rely on globally integrated production networks and how much of the value added embodied in trade flows is created in different countries.

Table 3.3 Double counting exports

	Raw materials	Processing	Manufacture	Final consumption	Gross exports	Domestic value added	Double counting of value added
Country 1	5				5	5	0
Country 2		5+5=10			10	5	5
Country 3			10+5=15		15	5	10
Country 4				15			
				Sum	30	15	15

SUMMARY

In this chapter we discussed the changing geography of production with the capitalist market economy. We explored reasons for the existence of firms and changes in the organization of production and its geography, and outlined the conditions under which some firms become TNCs. The growth of TNCs and their significance within the global economy was tracked through analysis of FDI and through data reporting TNC-related trade and employment.

These data suggest that the global system of trade is not one that is best understood by the arms-length exchanges of firms that produce their goods and services in one country and then export them around the world. The contemporary global economy is largely shaped by the activities of TNCs that have fragmented research, production and marketing operations across multiple partners located in many different countries. This reality raises questions about the usefulness of orthodox trade theory to explain the spatial organization of global production patterns and trade today.

It should be clear from the discussion above that the GPNs managed by TNCs assemble and link pools of capital, labor and other resources in different parts of the world economy. The importance of various inputs to production, their substitutability and their relative mobility ties segments of production networks to particular locations. Insofar as different places (sets of workers, firms and broader institutions) can capture these segments, they lock in economic growth for shorter or longer periods of time. However, the constant march of competition, and more rapid shifts in technology and demand, mean that fewer and fewer places are secure in terms of their long-run futures. In this dynamic environment, the ability of state institutions to craft effective trade policy and trap economic growth is increasingly difficult. It is to these issues that we turn in the next two chapters.

The main points of this chapter are:

- The origins of the global economy are closely intertwined with the emergence of TNCs. These are corporations that own or control production operations across international borders.

- Following Dunning, a firm will become a TNC when it generates ownership-specific advantages, when it chooses to internalize these advantages and when it decides to prosecute its advantages in a foreign location.
- The growth of TNCs has been extremely rapid over the last few decades. This has resulted in the fragmentation of production processes and their integration in complex networks or value chains that tie workers, firms and entire nations to the global economy.
- A growing share of world trade and capital flows is dominated by the activities of TNCs.

SUGGESTED READING

The website of the Global Policy Forum has a number of papers on globalization and TNCs (listed under Social and Economic Policy, available at https://www.globalpolicy.org/home.html)

UNCTAD runs a journal devoted to TNC activities (available at http://unctad.org/en/Pages/DIAE/Research%20on%20FDI%20and%20TNCs/Transnational-Corporations-Journal.aspx)

RESOURCES

For measuring value-added trade, you may wish to check out:

IDE-JETRO: http://www.ide.go.jp/English/Data/index.html

OECD/WTO: http://www.oecd.org/sti/ind/measuringtradeinvalue-addedanoecd-wtojointinitiative.htm

UNCTAD-Eora GVC Database at http://unctad.org/en/PublicationsLibrary/diae2013d1_en.pdf

The UNCTAD website (http://unctad.org) contains many resources on globalization, FDI and the activities of TNCs. See the annual World Investment Report.

The Food and Agriculture Organization (FAO) provides a nice overview of how to conduct value chain analysis. (Available at www.fao.org/docs/up/easypol/935/value_chain_analysis_fao_vca_software_tool_methodological_guidelines_129en.pdf)

The Global Value Chains Initiative at Duke University provides a great deal of information on value chain analysis. See https://globalvaluechains.org

Free.sourcemap.com and Sourcemap.org provide additional information on supply chain analysis and mapping.

Global exchange is an international human rights organization focused on processes of globalization and their impacts. See www.globalexchange.org

4

TRADE GOVERNANCE

In his 1988 State of the Union address, American President Ronald Reagan declared that: "We should always remember: Protectionism is destructionism. America's jobs, America's growth, America's future depend on trade—trade that is free, open, and fair". American presidents after Reagan have generally embraced free trade in their foreign policies. Yet, for most of the eighteenth and nineteenth centuries, the US was described by Paul Bairoch (1993) to be "the mother country and bastion of modern protectionism" (p. 30). Distance from Europe and Asia, together with its sizeable domestic market, contributed to this state of affairs. Trade policy demands from different sectors of the US economy were mixed. On the one hand, industrialists in the northeast of the country desired protection for their manufactured products. On the other hand, farmers in the south, faced with a global over-supply, experienced declining prices for their exports and were against protectionism. The industrialists won and the US implemented the Smoot–Hawley Tariff Act in 1930 that saw an unprecedented level of restrictions on imports from both the agricultural and manufacturing sectors. In turn, some twenty-five countries retaliated against the US by raising their own trade barriers, and international trade collapsed, deepening the Great Depression.

In this chapter, we describe the rationales as well as instruments of protectionism, institutional theories and the forms of governance created to prevent trade policy from returning to the protectionism of the 1930s. As the Bairoch quote suggests, it is hard to find any country that truly practices free trade. Both England and France came close to practicing free trade in the mid-nineteenth century, but tariffs, though low, were never completely eliminated. For this reason, much of the concern today is directed at achieving freer trade through governance mechanisms, specifically institutions. The largest and most developed of these institutions is the World Trade Organization (WTO). Smaller and more limited attempts to open trade have also been made through bilateral and regional free trade arrangements between two or more countries.

INSTITUTIONAL THEORIES

If protectionism harms trade as free trade champions have claimed, then trade liberalization, that is the elimination of tariffs and other related barriers, should achieve the opposite effect (see Box 4.1). In the wake of the calamitous contraction of world trade following the

BOX 4.1 Barrier to trade

Tariffs are the most common form of barriers to trade. They act like a tax and are custom duties that are imposed by a country on foreign imports. Duties may be specific by fixing the amount to a unit of imported good: for example, US$20 per ton of the imported commodity. Another type of tariff is the ad valorem tariff. Here the tax is calculated as a percentage of the value of the imported good. A third type of tariff combines both the specific tax and ad valorem tariff, and is called the compound tariff. For many countries, tariffs are applied to help protect domestic industries although they can also be a source of revenue for developing countries. Industries are protected when suppliers or citizens find it relatively more expensive to purchase inputs or goods that are imported than local inputs and goods.

Non-tariff barriers (NTBs) are more difficult to define. As the term implies, they are all other barriers that are not considered to be tariffs (Deardorff and Stern, 1998). The most common NTBs are export subsidies, import quotas and voluntary export restraints (VERs). When governments offer payments that help an industry to export its products, this is an export subsidy. Such a subsidy is commonly found in the agricultural sector of industrialized countries. European sugar producers are guaranteed minimum prices on sugar beets which are grown in Northern Europe. Such an action is unfavorably viewed because it artificially increases the income of European sugar producers. The second type of NTBs, import quotas, occurs when a country limits the amount of goods that may be imported from another country for a period of time. The textile industry of the United States has long complained about the displacement of American workers from imports of foreign textiles. The US government has responded to the complaints by imposing quotas on textile and apparel products from China. As the *New York Times* has pointed out, even baby cotton diapers were affected, resulting in higher priced diapers. Finally, the third type of NTBs is voluntary export restraint. Here, the exporting country voluntarily agrees to limit its quantity of specific exports to the importing country to avoid retaliation. VERs can also occur in the form of export forecasts. Japan's implementation of VERs in the 1980s and 1990s involved both forms of VERS, that is restricting quantities of its passenger cars to the US, as well as providing export forecasts to both Canada and the EU.

In addition to the above, NTBs can include informal barriers that are created by culture. For example, cultural institutions may favor domestic over foreign industries. Some western countries for instance believe that Japan's industrial networks act as cultural barriers because they help to minimize foreign competition and imports. This issue will be taken up in the next chapter.

Smoot–Hawley Tariff Act, the US and UK were anxious to prevent economic harm of this magnitude again and worked together to establish an international organization that would promote trade liberalization. The General Agreement on Trade and Tariffs (GATT) was the result of this effort. In order to appreciate the raison d'être of GATT and its successor, the WTO, we need to understand the theoretical arguments for institution-building. For this, we draw largely from a political–economy perspective to obtain relevant insights.

Trading internationally involves interactions between economic agents (e.g. organizations and firms), and between elites from different states or countries. In this section, we will use the term "state" rather than country to describe transnational trading interactions. This is because a state denotes some element of agency since it encompasses individuals, usually political and government elites, who are endowed with the authority (through the holding of office) to make decisions that impact society. Interactions between states are prone to conflict because states embody economic agents that are in competition with one another, because they differ geographically in terms of resources, market access and the information they possess. Geographical differences mean that states operate with some level of uncertainty about the international environment in the trading of goods and services. Response to uncertainty varies depending on a state's interest and pressures from domestic groups and this potentially opens up space for trade conflict. Institutional theory offers a theoretical rationale for explaining how trade conflicts may be reduced since institutions enable interactions to be structured in ways such that behavior may be more predictable.

The most popular way of defining an institution is that it consists of a set of norms and rules that describe and prescribe the behavioral roles of a group of actors. Norms may be informal, developing out of a set of cultural practices that are geographically embedded in a network of social relationships. Norms can also be formal assuming a bureaucratic character of distinctive forms, processes and competences (Selznick, 1996). When interactions are organized in a formal structure, they tend to be stable with relatively well-defined competency associated with a set of technical activities. Such stability may be traced to rules, often encoded in legal frameworks that stipulate how political elites and economic actors should interact with one another in the context of competition and cooperation. To be competent, an institution assumes a mode of governance or structure that channels its members to accomplish various goals. Explaining the motivation for forming an institution and benefits associated with institution-building, however, varies depending on the school of thought. We describe three such schools below.

The first school, neoliberalism, suggests that since the international market is characterized by high transaction costs, the goal of institutions is to reduce those costs (Keohane, 1984; North, 1990). As Chapter 3 indicates, transaction costs refer to the costs of gathering and monitoring information. Information costs are high when a country undertakes trade with a foreign country that is different in tastes and culture. They can also be high when it is difficult to monitor information related to the quality of goods imported from a foreign supplier. By providing a set of rules through agreements, treaties or established norms, information can be increased to members of institutions. In turn, transaction costs are lowered.

Proponents of the neoliberal school believe that states act in their own self-interest. This prevents them from developing common interests. By forming institutions, they will enjoy the benefits of decreased transaction costs through a reduction of uncertainty. One major benefit of institutionalizing interactions is that increased information flow will promote a process of learning among elite officials and economic actors about the advantages of multilateralism over domestic interests and social practices. Learning results in a shared mental model that stabilizes interactions through the development of routines, procedures and solutions (Mantzavinos et al., 2004). The overall outcome is positive because members learn to adopt cooperation over conflict.

The second school, neofunctionalism, may be traced to the 1960s but has recently witnessed a resurgence (Cini and Borragan, 2013). The theory proposes that institutions facilitate the larger goal of regional integration between states. Take the example of European Union (EU) integration. As globalization expanded in the 1960s, economic problems also became more transnational: for example, international trade, food safety and environmental pollution, which demanded new transnational solutions (these issues are elaborated in Chapter 6). Neofunctionalists see the organization of states into a supranational community or society to be one such solution. But getting states to relinquish their national sovereignty is not an easy task. Hence neofunctionalists propose jumpstarting the process by organizing key economic functions of the state through supranational agencies. Over time, these agencies develop competencies from the tasks and authority entrusted to them. This in turn will initiate a process of spillover where economic activities in one region or state influence the economic activities of another region or state. When spillovers expand geographically, regions or states also become more interconnected from increased spatial integration of economic functions and activities. Transnational region-building is encouraged and states will begin to shift the geographical scale of their loyalties from national to the continental in keeping with the emergence of a supranational community.

Agencies and organizations become institutionalized when interactions evolve from loose couplings to a more predictable pattern. That is to say, institution-building involves socialization where interactions are transformed from a loose to a stable pattern. Socialization refers to the process where actors begin to adopt new norms of a community or group gradually internalizing the rules that are associated with these norms. For neofunctionalists, socialization encourages political and economic elites and officials not only to develop competency at a transnational level, but also to forge shared understanding that scales up identity-formation beyond the domestic or national level. Institutions are ultimately expected to perform an enabling role by facilitating the establishment of agreements that arise from the interactions.

The third school, constructivism—often called the new institutionalism—is also interested in the nature of social interactions that result in learning and socialization. Institutions are seen to be ideational, not just material structures. Rules and norms are not only treaties and agreements, but are formed from the ideas of individuals within an institution. How ideas are exchanged and translated requires attention to communication patterns between actors and their discourses (Ruggie, 1998). Communication is realized through acts of deliberation and negotiation, and these in turn promote learning and socialization. Because of the theory's interest in the nature of social interactions and communication of ideas, socialization features much more prominently in this school than the theory of neofunctionalism. Institutions matter because they are sites where ideas may be communicated, contested and learned (Checkel, 2005). For example, international institutions such as the WTO are made up of groups of officials and representatives in the form of councils, panels and committees from member countries. They work out WTO agreements and are responsible for distilling trade issues from agriculture, subsidies to market access and financial services. Agreement is discursively produced in that it involves iterations of arguments, challenges, persuasions and texts. Committee members are placed in settings where contact is prolonged. Extended periods of contact and communication stimulate adaptation to new roles, or they trigger a new understanding of interests and identities that help move officials and elites towards a convergence of supranational community norms. The constructivist approach highlights the dynamics, nature and loci of social interactions that are thought to shape institutional formation.

Overall, the three schools discussed above provide complementary theoretical explanations for governing trade exchanges and relations between states and actors through the mechanism of institutions. However, since institutions can be informal or formal, the form they assume depends on the geography of the environment. A less normative view such as constructivism is more likely to favor understanding the particular nature of social interactions from one region to another, while a more normative theory like neofunctionalism presumes that supranational institutions in European integration may be universally applied. Yet states in East and Southeast Asia have rejected a neofunctional or neoliberal model of geographical integration for many years. They favor a more informal form of institutionalization reflecting their societies' makeup of close-knit groups and emphasis of personal relationships. Here, cultural norms shape expectations, and networks of personal entanglements serve as a major conduit of information flow. In contrast, western industrialized countries prefer formal institutions as a mechanism to solve transnational problems and conflicts in trade. They believe that rules, typically articulated in a legal framework, are more likely to enlist the cooperation of states to work towards multilateralism. This belief has led to the creation of an international institution, namely the WTO and its predecessor GATT, to regulate and stabilize trade interactions in the world while meeting the primary goal of freer multilateral trade.

GATT AND WTO

The last sixty years have witnessed a concerted effort to create incentives and to establish institutions that would move inter-country trade in the direction towards freer rather than restricted trade. Among them, the World Bank (the International Bank for Reconstruction and Development) and International Monetary Fund (IMF) were established to promote economic development, free trade and exchange rate stability. The principal institutions for realizing multilateral free trade, however, are the GATT and the WTO.

General Agreement on Tariffs and Trade (GATT)

In 1947, the US invited twenty-two other countries for a round of trade talks concerning the reduction of tariffs in Geneva. The aim was to try and convince these countries to adopt an institutional framework where countries would cooperate to lower trade barriers as a step toward more open trade. At that time, the US was the largest exporter accounting for one-third of world exports followed at some distance (12.2% of world exports) by the United Kingdom (Kim, 2010). The US was in a strong position to convince the other countries to work towards freer trade, not least because of the central role played by the US in the postwar Bretton Woods accord. To secure such a framework, the countries agreed to more closely coordinate trade relations among three or more states around a set of norms and rules rather than to conduct trade through the more popular bilateral agreements that were in operation at that time. Institutional scholars consider a multilateral trading system to be superior because a bilateral mode diminishes the ability of smaller and less powerful nations to negotiate. This multilateral trading model became the foundation for how free trade was to be achieved in subsequent years.

As elaborated in the previous section, industrialized countries in the west favored achieving multilateralism through the formal institutionalization of interactions between states. At a minimum, this would involve consultation or specific agreements and treaties between governments. The result of the 1947 talk in Geneva was the establishment of such agreements known as GATT. Initially, GATT was conceived as part of a more comprehensive framework, through the establishment of the International Trade Organization (ITO) to achieve multilateral trade. However, the ITO never materialized while GATT gained momentum. From the previous section, we know that one objective of institution-building is to create norms and expectations in a stable and predictable space that facilitates interactions between parties. To promote this goal, GATT operated around three principles. First it would be an economically liberal regime. Upon accession, members are expected to practice economic openness through the free exchange of goods and services with other members. Second, the most-favored-nation (MFN) status requires that the same favorable tariff and regulatory treatment granted to one member be extended to all other members as well. This is to develop a norm of non-discrimination status among all members. The final reciprocity principle advances the idea that a member should reduce its tariff in exchange for similar reciprocal concessions from its trading partner. Here, members are expected to "balance out" the exchange of benefits based on the value of trade (Barton et al., 2006).

At its core, the GATT comprises a set of rules and agreements that make up the multilateral trading system. Its institutional foundation is not as deep as its successor the WTO as there was no automatic process to resolve trade disputes nor to discipline errant practices. Indeed, GATT contained many loopholes and escape clauses for countries that were hesitant to embrace its principles. Four examples of loopholes are briefly highlighted. First, according to Article XIX, trade restrictions may be reinstated if imports cause harm to a country's domestic industry. Second, Article VI permits extra tariffs to be applied to offset dumping when imports are sold at less than the sale price of products in the home country. Third, GATT also made provisions under Article XXIV for the formation of a customs union. Finally, developing countries were thought to have special needs because their markets and industries were less developed. They were permitted to exercise the principle of non-reciprocity where tariff reductions negotiated with developed countries need not be balanced by reciprocal commitments to those countries. These loopholes were tolerated for a few years when the size of membership was relatively small. The original twenty-three GATT countries accounted for nearly three-quarters of world trade in the late 1940s, and they shared relatively similar goals of trade liberalization. Trade relations were not so complicated given the small membership size, and most of the negotiations focused on merchandise trade and tariffs. In general, the GATT evolved through a series of trade rounds beginning with Geneva. Some of the rounds lasted several years. The last round, The Uruguay Round, which began in 1986 and ended in 1994, was perhaps the most comprehensive; it also set the stage for the establishment of the WTO. Among the issues discussed, reform of the dispute settlement process was a major preoccupation. Countries disagreed on the surveillance and monitoring of prodecures and rules. Japan, for example, was concerned about possible interference in their trade policies. However, the US was eager to see greater institutional coherence having been engaged in a series of long-standing disputes with other countries, for example the EU–US beef hormone dispute (see Box 4.2). Hence the US pushed for deeper formal institutionalization to enhance decision-making.

BOX 4.2 EU–US beef hormone dispute

Since 1981, the European Union, then the European Community (EC), has been prohibiting trade on livestock raised with growth hormones. DES (dethylstiboestrol) contamination in veal production, for example, had led to a massive boycott of meat by European consumers in the 1970s. To stem the erosion of consumer confidence, the European Commission called for a ban on livestock raised with non-therapeutic hormones. This ban largely impacted the beef industry in North America, which uses hormones to help cattle grow faster and to increase the protein content of meat. After considerable debates and reports from scientific committees, the European Parliament decided to ban all growth hormone meat imports despite the Commission's advice to permit use of three natural hormones in 1988.

Hard hit by the ban, the US took the case up with the General Agreement on Tariffs and Trade (GATT) and requested a technical committee be formed to examine their complaint. This request was blocked by GATT's contracting parties. Consequently, the US retaliated against the EC ban by slapping on a number of European agricultural imports with 100% ad valorem duties worth about $100 million. In turn, the EC requested a panel from GATT to look into the matter but this was blocked by the US. The hormone beef dispute demonstrates why countries moved ahead to form the World Trade Organization (WTO): GATT's institutional structure favored diplomacy and lacked the ability to handle contracting parties' (usually a country) blockages as this chapter suggests. As the European ban took effect in 1989, trans-Atlantic trade on meat exploded into a trade war. The standoff only began to whittle down in the mid-1990s with the establishment of the WTO. Under the WTO's Dispute Settlement Understanding, countries or contracting parties could no longer block a ruling or request a hearing panel as easily as the GATT regime permitted. This represented an opportunity to re-focus the dispute on rules that were more predictable. Today the long-standing hormone beef trade war remains only partially resolved: the EU has agreed to raise its imports of North American beef, particularly non-hormone treated beef, and the US and Canada have suspended duties on black-listed luxury European agricultural products that had been part of their retaliation. But the EU ban on hormone beef remains in place.

World Trade Organization

By the 1980s globalization had grown considerably deeper and broader. Intellectual shifts were friendly to new logics of protectionism. In 1988, the US enacted Super 301 aimed at forcing the opening of foreign markets. Multilateral trade appeared to be retreating. What GATT lacked were formalized rules and laws that could more satisfactorily address the growing complexities of trade issues. These complexities include agriculture, services and intellectual property rights. Application of Super 301 forced European countries and Japan to be more willing to put aside their reservations regarding institutional reforms. In 1990, Italy proposed the establishment of an institution that would supervise the GATT system. This new institution would be characterized by a legal character, and it would host a strong secretariat (Stiles, 1996). With the adoption of the Italian proposal, the path was paved for the creation of the WTO.

With much fanfare, the WTO was established in 1995 and has steadily expanded its membership since then. As of 2015, some 161 economies have become members of the WTO. There are several differences between GATT and the WTO. First, whereas GATT confined itself to merchandise trade and tariffs only, the WTO expanded its menu of trade items to include non-tariff barriers, agriculture, services, investment and intellectual property. Second, as noted earlier, GATT operated more like a series of agreements between diplomats, and a panel report issued as the result of a complaint could be blocked by the offending party. The dispute mechanism was changed in keeping with a more formal and legalistic mode of interactions in the WTO: a unanimous decision is now needed to block a report. Disputes are pursued under a unified dispute settlement mechanism (DSM). This includes services and intellectual property, which eliminates confusion over which procedure to use for different issues. It also helps to minimize long delays that tended to occur under GATT. Moreover, once the panel issues its report, there are procedures for complying with the rulings of the report that did not happen in GATT. Third, all members must accept the multilateral trade agreements from the Uruguay Rounds under its "single undertaking" principle. This includes developing countries, which under GATT were not obliged to follow all codes of conduct developed in the agreements. Fourth, since the WTO is run by member governments, typically trade ministers, they are expected to convene more frequently, that is once every two years, in meetings that interpret or translate WTO agreements.

The WTO has led to a more efficient system of handling trade conflicts. Other benefits of the WTO include the general lowering of average tariffs for manufacturing exports, deterrents on implementing trade policies that might harm other countries, and the tackling of newer, more complex trade-related issues in services and intellectual property (Deardorff and Stern, 2000). However, the WTO has also been heavily criticized. Because of its formal structure, the WTO disadvantages developing countries that are not familiar with western legal institutions and their form of social interactions. Among civil groups like environmental and labor activists, the WTO is perceived to be a country club that ignores environmental fallout from trade and the neglect of labor standards by corporations. These are issues that we will take up further in Chapter 6. Furthermore, institutions that formalize human interactions in a series of legal transactions are generally viewed less favorably among Asian nations. In trade disputes between Japan and South Korea with the US, for example, Asian countries are hesitant to enter into legal action but prefer bilateral dialogues to build confidence instead (Yoshimatsu, 2003). Overall, the WTO is both ardently supported and bitterly criticized.

GEOGRAPHY OF TRADE: INTEGRATION AND REGIONAL TRADE AGREEMENTS

Despite the dispersing forces of globalization, studies show that the dominant pattern of world trade is not one of dispersion but that of regionalization where trade is occurring between proximate countries that are circumscribed by regional boundaries (Kohl and Brouwer, 2014; Poon, 1997; Poon et al., 2000). In geography, theorization of region has tended to favor the subnational scale; hence regionalism generally refers to regional development processes that occur at the local scale. In this chapter, regionalism is examined at the supranational level and the unit of analysis is a country or state. Economic development is typically conceived as occurring in a container space hosting resources, labor and capital that are inputs of the production process. Such a space or region tends to assume a discrete nature that is associated with relatively homogenous functions. For example, a trade region is defined by trade functions. The containerization of space is the most popular way of describing regions among political scientists and economists. However, geographers observe that regions today are no longer so self-contained and many of them are engaged in extra-regional interactions establishing networks that link different spatial units (Poon et al., 2000). They argue that the region is not a coherent homogenous territory with a fixed boundary but a semi-coherent unit that is subjected to global networks of economic flows (e.g. trade) as well as spatial tendencies towards discretization (Jonas, 2012).

While European regionalism has pursued the goal of economic integration beyond trade, elsewhere in the world the picture is rather different. In East Asia, countries have increased their levels of trade with one another, yet they have not pursued deeper integration goals like their European counterparts. That is to say, regionalization of trade has not been accompanied by regionalism. The terms regionalism and regionalization should therefore be distinguished: whereas regionalism typically arises from regionalization, the reverse may not be true. Regionalism in Europe has worked towards political patterns of coordination, cooperation and territorial politics, but regionalization in East Asia has not translated into a similar outcome.

Adding to the variety of scales at which countries are trading with one another (global and regional) is that of bilateralism. This refers to trade between two countries or states. Bilateral trade is the most common geographical mode of trade interaction. The United States has a trilateral free trade area involving two other countries, that is Mexico and Canada. But it has in place some twenty bilateral trade agreements with countries from Latin America, Asia and the Middle East. What accounts for the popularity of bilateral free trade agreements (FTAs) which remove trade barriers between members? One explanation lies in geographical proximity: most FTAs are forged between neighboring states reflecting lower transaction costs between them. Neighbors are more likely to be acquainted and to be more knowledgeable about each other's markets, culture and language. The world's largest bilateral trade partnership is between the US and Canada. But proximity is not the only reason for bilateral agreements; other factors also matter, such as political considerations. A case in point is South Korea, which has forged an FTA with a rather distant partner, Chile, for political reasons. In this case, objections by farmers over the FTA may be circumvented because Chile's summer growing season for agricultural products will not directly compete with farmers since it is then winter in Korea.

IS GEOGRAPHY DESTINY? REGIONALISM AND REGIONAL ECONOMIC INTEGRATION

There are four stages of regional economic integration. The lowest level of integration is the free trade area and agreement (FTA). Here participating states agree to reduce a range of products that offer members preferential access to their markets. The North American Free Trade Agreement (NAFTA) is one such example. When member states decide to establish both a common internal tariff among themselves as well as external tariffs with third parties, regional economic integration is moved up a notch to become a customs union (CU). MERCOSUR's four original founding members, Argentina, Brazil, Paraguay (currently suspended) and Uruguay, decided to form a CU in 2008 to eliminate barriers to trade. In the third stage, countries begin to pursue economic union through coordination of monetary and technical policies. The final and highest stage of integration is political integration.

FTAs are the most popular stage of regional economic integration among countries. The WTO lists some 583 negotiated regional FTAs of which 377 are in force. At this level of economic integration, countries need only agree on a common level of tariff reduction and this is relatively easy to achieve. Ceding sovereignty at higher levels of integration is still viewed with suspicion by many countries, as Brexit has demonstrated. There is also the geographical factor. One prerequisite for the success of a regional FTA is that trade among the members should already be relatively high before the agreement, and this tends to be the case between neighboring states.

European Union: Super-region?

The best example of regionalism is the EU, which has advanced furthest in the level of regional economic integration. Early on, neofunctional theory laid out the foundation for how state actors could purposively proceed with continental integration, while neoliberalism lent support by substantiating the economic logic of such integration. However, the theories ran into some trouble in the early 1990s when European integration was stalled by a few events. Chief among them was the defeat of the referendums associated with the 1992 Maastricht Treaty by Danish voters. The Maastricht Treaty was formulated to move Europe to monetary and economic union. After its defeat, the Treaty was amended and then resurrected in 1997 as the Treaty on the EU that outlined goals for political union (Laursen, 2008). Region-building is a complex process and globalization in the 1990s had brought to fore many issues that were not apparent in the previous decades. The rise of East Asia and China, for instance, meant that Europe could not ignore extra-regional linkages. Encouraged by increased freedom of mobility, in-migration across the continent generated backlash among local communities. Contradictions between globalization and regionalism meant that the latter needed to be negotiated between citizens, civil society, business and political elites. To understand the shift in the framing of Europe, we chronicle the history of European integration below (Table 4.1)

The birth of the EU may be traced to 1951 when a group of six countries, namely Belgium, France, Italy, Luxembourg, the Netherlands and West Germany decided to form the European Coal and Steel Community (ECSC). The goal of ECSC was to free the flow and trade of raw materials, specifically coal and steel, in heavy industries. Both materials were central inputs to Europe's industrialization at that time. By 1957, the EU began to take shape when the six countries signed the Treaty of Rome that provided the foundation for creating the European Economic Community (EEC). Essentially, the Treaty developed beyond the movement of coal and steel to a timetable of free trade and economic cooperation in a number of sectors. The first step was to form a CU where members would eliminate tariffs among themselves and with third parties. Member states also agreed to a common agricultural policy that would guarantee prices for farmers as well as a regional development policy that targeted poor regions. The next step, to be achieved in twelve years, was to establish a common market that encompassed four economic freedoms—freedom of goods, services, capital and people. In actual fact, the common market would become a reality only in 1986 under the SEA. In the next step, the EEC would develop common economic policies in agriculture, transportation

Table 4.1 Timeline of the formation of the European Union

1951:	Belgium, France, Italy, Luxembourg, the Netherlands and West Germany form the European Coal and Steel Community (ECSC)
1957:	Treaty of Rome is signed to establish the EEC
1968:	Customs union is formed among the original six founding members
1973:	Denmark, Ireland and the United Kingdom join
1981:	Greece joins
1986:	Portugal and Spain join the EEC Single European Act to form the common market is signed EEC is called the European Community (EC)
1992:	Maastricht Treaty is signed to establish economic and monetary union (EMU) European Community is called the European Union (EU) Danish voters reject the Maastricht Treaty
1993:	Danish voters approve the Maastricht Treaty with some amendments
1995:	Austria, Finland and Sweden join
1999:	Introduction of the Euro currency and EMU
2004:	Cyprus, Czech Republic, Estonia, Latvia, Lithuania, Hungary, Malta, Poland, Slovenia and Slovakia join Treaty of European Constitution signed
2005:	Dutch and French votes reject the European Constitution Period of "reflection" to follow
2007:	Bulgaria and Romania join Treaty of Lisbon is signed following amendments of the European Constitution
2013:	Croatia joins, completing EU-28
2016:	UK votes to exit EU (Brexit)

and industry with the aim of protecting worker welfare. To facilitate decision-making, the Treaty created five institutions, namely the European Council, European Commission, European Parliament, European Court of Justice and the European Court of Auditors (described in Box 4.3). These institutions have largely governed the process of EU development although they have been subjected to some reforms.

With the Treaty of Rome, the way was paved for greater regionalism when the CU became a reality in 1968 among the original six founding members. As the integration movement gathered momentum, enlargement of membership also began to take place. Membership expanded in 1973 when three countries,

BOX 4.3 Main institutions of the European Union

The three pillars of European Union (EU) institutions are the European Council, European Commission and European Parliament.

The European Council (also known as the Council of Ministers) comprises government heads that represent each member state's government. The Council is the legislative arm of the EU and makes the final decisions on all legislative proposals. Because of its decision-making power, it is responsible for EU policy and political discussions, priorities and direction. In general, the Council is responsible for EU governance through its coordination of economic and fiscal matters, implementation of foreign and security matters, and the approval and signing of international agreements and treaty proposals from the European Commission. Much of its work is done through thousands of national officials in working groups tasked with looking over proposals at early stages of negotiation.

The European Commission is the second major EU institution. While called a Commission, it is really a college of commissioners because it is made up of the twenty-eight members representing the EU-28, and each commissioner is assigned an area of policy and service portfolio. In this sense, the Commission is responsible for the day-to-day running of the EU. It proposes and drafts legislation, and assesses the potential impacts of economic, social and environmental outcomes of new proposals. It is involved in the policy-making process from the beginning to the end. While the European Council and Parliament can also propose legislation, it is the task of the Commission to examine these proposals through consultation with the twenty-eight members, the business community, trade unions and other relevant actors. Following the Treaty of Lisbon, the Commission has been given greater power to monitor members' compliance of EU laws and to pursue sanctions that are legally binding (Andersen, 2012). In this sense, the Commission may be said to be the guardian and enforcer of treaties.

The third institution is the European Parliament. The Parliament is distinguished from the two institutions above in that it is designed to represent the interest of European citizens. Members are elected by EU voters every five years. Because membership is roughly based on population size, a large country like Germany has nearly 100 Parliament members. The Parliament essentially plays three roles, approval of the appointment of the twenty-eight commissioners, scrutiny of EU laws and amending the Commission's legislation proposals (Cini and Borragan, 2013). The last function means that it serves as a check on the

Commission through scrutiny of the latter's reports. Because it is designed to represent citizens' interest, the public can initiate petitions to the Parliament which in turn will set up committees to examine the petitions. In this sense, the Parliament exercizes power of scrutiny over the executive.

In addition to the three institutions above, two other instititions deserve to be mentioned. They are the European Court of Justice and the European Court of Auditors. The European Court of Justice supports legislation through its power to interpret EU law, settle disputes and sanction infringement or non-compliance of regulations and laws between EU governments and institutions. Finally the European Court of Auditors helps to manage the finances of the EU by auditing persons or organizations involved in the use or disbursement of EU funds.

Denmark, Ireland and the United Kingdom (UK), joined the EEC. Greece soon followed (1981), along with Portugal and Spain (1986), Austria, Finland and Sweden (1995), Cyprus, Czech Republic, Estonia, Latvia, Lithuania, Hungary, Malta, Poland, Slovenia and Slovakia (2004), Bulgaria and Romania (2007), and finally Croatia (2013). Today the twenty-eight members of EU are commonly referred to as EU-28 (Table 4.1).

Economic integration was given further life when France initiated efforts to create a single market through a new treaty, the Single European Act (SEA), which became effective in 1987. The SEA was more ambitious because it aimed to replace national regulations with pan-European regulations. By the early 1990s, the countries were confronted with new issues associated with freer regional trade, increased global competition, and greater mobility of capital and labor. The 1992 Maastricht Treaty sought not only to define citizenship rights for member countries (e.g. the right to work in the EEC) and cooperation between governments of member states on security and foreign policies, but also to complete economic and monetary union (EMU) through the introduction of a single currency, the Euro, in 1999 (Kahn, 2008). Danish voters' lack of enthusiasm reflected their discontent with the push for a new European citizenry with which they struggled to identify. Following amendments, it was nonetheless ratified in 1993. This, and further revisions in 1997 with the Treaty of Amsterdam, which added new objectives that seek to solve unemployment and gender inequality, paved the way for the single currency in 1999. A common currency is believed to positively affect trade by reducing uncertainty related to exchange rate volatility.

While the single monetary market strengthened the case for European monetary union, the EEC (by this time known as the EU) entered the new millennium facing an uncertain future. A key reason for the uncertainty was regional expansion into Eastern Europe. There were certain advantages in having Eastern Europe join the EU including increased investment to areas where labor costs were cheaper. These advantages were exploited in the production networks of the automobile industry linking German and East European producers. The entry of post-socialist economies intensified efforts to impose a legal character on the Union, to reinforce human rights and freedoms, and to protect health and the environment (see Box 4.2). The legal thrust meant that there was a need to establish a European Constitution that would help transform regulations into laws. Signed in 2004, the Treaty that established the European Constitution was nonetheless defeated, this time by Dutch and French voters in 2005. According to a survey by the European Commission, Dutch voters listed "lack of information" and "loss of national sovereignty" as their top two reasons for rejecting the Constitution (Eurobarometer, 2005). Two years later at Lisbon, it was ratified following amendments to strengthen institutions such as the European Parliament and to address democratic deficits that the public had voiced. More importantly, it abandoned the constitutional idea of its 2004 predecessor, which would have given a greater weight to European than national laws (Chalmers et al., 2010). With this, progress in regionalism was restored because the 2007 Treaty of Lisbon stabilized decades of negotiations over the forms and institutional governance structure of the Union. More importantly, from a trade viewpoint, the Treaty made provisions for clearer rules not just on goods, but on services (e.g. health and education) and intellectual property rights as well.

Nonetheless, it is not difficult to see that European integration has not been a smooth process. In 2015, Greece had some trouble meeting its debt obligations to the European Commission, European

Central Bank and IMF. This resulted in capital control and the closure of banks. Greek officials complained that stiff bailout conditions hurt their citizens far too much. By defaulting on its loans, Greece became a candidate for exiting the EU. Citizens in favor of a Greek exit believed that this would offer the country greater monetary control to design its own destiny. A year later, similar concerns of a loss of border control triggered the British vote against EU membership. Clearly, neofunctional and neoliberal theories did not predict the defeats of the 1992 Maastricht Treaty, the 2004 Treaty of European Union, or Greek and British unease about EU membership. Advantages of efficiency with integration did not always trump citizens' concerns over what it means to be European when economic and political affairs are scaled up geographically beyond the national level. Indeed one criticism of neofunctional theory is that it advocates a regionalism that is top-down, a normative framework that is implemented by political elites. But as the Brexit suggests, a top-down approach fails to adequately accommodate citizens' concerns of adverse effects that greater integration could bring. The current popularity of the new institutional constructivist perspective lies in its attention to the construction of identities and shared meanings across wider population segments and groups. Questions of identity continue to occupy much of the research on the EU today.

North American Free Trade Agreement

In 1990, newly elected President Carols Salinas de Gortari from Mexico approached US president George Bush about the possibility of forming a free trade area. Together with Canada's then prime minister, Brian Mulroney, discussions between the three countries regarding the lowering of trade barriers led to a historic treaty, the 1994 NAFTA.

Until then, Mexico was engaged in an industrialization strategy of import-substitution that replaced exports with domestic imports (see Chapter 5). However, President Salinas wanted to steer the country away from an over-dependence on oil exports and to diversify the economy to manufactured exports. This meant attracting foreign direct investment that would raise the quality of Mexican manufactured exports to a world standard (Baer, 1991). Since the US constitutes an important market for both investment and manufactured exports, securing an FTA could help ensure access for Mexico's exports. The FTA was also part of the president's plan to gradually liberalize the Mexican economy through sectoral restructuring. Armed with a team of technocrats who were trained in the United States, President Salinas sought to reverse decades of economic nationalism by opening the country up to American imports and markets with the trade agreement.

As for Canada, it had earlier implemented an FTA with the US in 1989 when it was brought into the NAFTA discussion. Mexico was not an important market and trade with the country was relatively low: exports to and imports from Mexico were less than 0.5% and 1.25% of its total exports and imports respectively in 1989 (Watson, 1992). Public opinion was against NAFTA as Canada was still facing anti-dumping actions by the Americans despite the Canada–US FTA, and the country was experiencing a deep recession. Canadian citizens were skeptical that NAFTA would solve cross-border trade conflicts and revive the economy. But the US was also Canada's largest trading partner, and the trade balance favored Canada that enjoyed trade surpluses with its southern neighbor. Moreover, production networks were becoming highly integrated across regions within the two countries, for example in the automobile industry. A significant volume of freight movement across the border involves intra-industry trade that is associated with the automobile industry. Besides this, Mexico and the US were going ahead with an FTA with or without Canada. Fearing trade diversion from Mexico, and despite opposition from labor unions, the Canadian prime minister signed the agreement.

Persuading congress and the American public to support NAFTA did not come easy in the United States. There were fears that cheaper goods resulting from Mexico's lower labor and environmental standards would flood the country. This aroused opposition from labor unions, environmental activists and industries worried about import competition. However, the end of the Uruguay Round was wrapping up with the US pressing aggressively for the opening up of markets for services, and protection of copyrights and patents. NAFTA presented an opportunity to obtain similar concessions from Canada and Mexico. American trade representatives negotiated a comprehensive set of trade rules that covered rules of origin (ROO), services, intellectual property and dispute settlement procedures.

Rules of origin, which determine if a product is foreign or domestic based on the country of origin, tend to be quite important in an FTA. For example, American negotiators wanted parts of the computer (e.g. motherboard, screen, hard disk) to be produced in the US. However, the US computer industry itself objected to this since many computer parts were imported from outside North America. Despite hard bargaining by the US, the agreement was concluded and became effective in 1994.

Studies of the impact of NAFTA, while mixed, have generally concluded that the agreement has increased trade among the three countries (Andressen, 2008). They show that Canada's exports to the US doubled in twelve years while also moving from low to high quality goods. NAFTA also transformed the economic geography of Canada from an east–west to a north–south axis. This implies that Canadian provinces, particularly Ontario and British Columbia, began trading more with the US than with other Canadian provinces. Crude petroleum is the largest US import from both Canada and Mexico. According to *The Economist* (2014), US trade increased faster with NAFTA countries (506%) than it did with non-NAFTA countries (279%) between 1993 and 2012. Data also suggest that the greatest beneficiary has been Mexico: domestic industries were able to upgrade themselves and become more productive while merchandise exports have penetrated the US market significantly. From the US perspective, NAFTA's effect on its economy is quite small, accounting for less than 5% of its gross domestic product (GDP) (Villarreal and Fergusson, 2014). This is because the domestic market is so large that much of its trade is domestic rather than international. Notwithstanding this, US trade with NAFTA members has tripled since 1994. Canada is the top export destination for some thirty-eight US states while Mexico is the main market for the exporters of another six states (Courchene, 2003). NAFTA also provided the US with a successful framework for FTA negotiations with other countries.

Overall, NAFTA has seen increased regionalization and some level of economic integration between the three countries. The automobile industry, for instance, is now so integrated that US automakers heavily use parts and components produced by the other two NAFTA countries. But NAFTA has also been criticized. It has led to the displacement of farmers, increased both income and regional disparities in Mexico, and overall trade and investment between Canada and Mexico remain low. More importantly, NAFTA members bear no ambition to be another EU pursuing a model of regionalization. As we will see below, such a model also describes regional integration in Southeast Asia.

The ASEAN way, AFTA and TPP

Like North America, countries in Southeast Asia have become increasingly integrated through trade and investment. Regionalism, however, has been slow to develop. There are some important differences between the countries here and those making up the EU and NAFTA. Nine of the ten Southeast Asian countries are developing economies and many are newly independent states that have emerged from long histories of colonialism.

Nascent regionalism in Southeast Asia may be traced to 1967 when five founding members, Indonesia, Malaysia, the Philippines, Singapore and Thailand, signed a declaration to form the Association of Southeast Asian Nations (ASEAN). This was considered to be a remarkable feat. Many of the countries had recently de-colonialized and nationalistic sentiments were high. The first couple of decades following de-colonialization were spent drawing boundaries that helped to consolidate national sovereignty. Constructing a regional community and identity were not priorities. ASEAN was born out of the necessity to cooperate on issues like security in a region where territorial disputes were not uncommon. Besides this, the countries wanted a larger bloc that would help them bargain on trade and investment issues with powerful countries like the United States. For the next twenty-seven years, ASEAN remained focused on issues that were related to regional peace and political stability. By 1984, it had expanded to six with the accession of Brunei Darussalam. Today, ASEAN comprises ten members following the addition of Vietnam (1995) Laos and Myanmar (1997) and Cambodia (1999).

In the early 1990s, it became clear that the EU was moving towards a single market while NAFTA was becoming an economic reality in North America. World trade was occurring around continental regions in spite of globalization. At this time, ASEAN members decided to form a free trade area, and the ASEAN free trade agreement (AFTA) was signed in 1992. This is considered by many

Table 4.2 Export share of the EU, NAFTA, AFTA and MERCOSUR, 1990 and 2013 (%)

	EU	NAFTA	AFTA	MERCOSUR
EU				
1990	60.5	8.2	1.5	0.6
2013	46.8	8.6	2.0	1.4
NAFTA				
1990	20.4	41.3	3.8	2.0
2013	12.0	49.2	3.6	3.5
AFTA				
1990	15.2	20.9	19.0	0.2
2013	8.7	10.2	25.8	0.9
MERCOSUR				
1990	25.8	32.7	2.5	7.6
2013	13.2	9.5	3.4	13.6

Source: IMF, Direction of Trade Statistics, various issues

Note: The figures refer to EC-12 members only

scholars to be a milestone in Asian regionalism. But the road to the FTA was bumpy. There are good reasons why AFTA took so long to form.

First, intra-regional trade is low. Table 4.2 shows the 1990 and 2013 intra-regional trade of AFTA compared to the EU and NAFTA. The largest volume of trade is between Singapore and Malaysia. Until recently, ASEAN countries tended to trade more with countries outside of the region than among themselves. Intra-regional trade was 19% in 1990, relatively low compared to 60.5% for the EU (Table 4.2). While intra-regional trade increased to nearly 26% in 2013, much of this is attributed to trade between just three countries—Indonesia, Singapore and Malaysia. These countries are responsible for nearly half of intra-AFTA trade. Given their high shares of extra-regional trade, the benefits of forming a free trade area were uncertain for ASEAN members.

Second, national sovereignty was a major concern. The countries were keen to pursue their own industrial and trade policies, and were suspicious of any regional arrangement that could impinge on those policies. Attempts at some level of economic coordination in the late 1970s through the ASEAN Industrial Projects (AIP) had turned out to be quite difficult. For example, Singapore wanted to build diesel engines through the AIP but this was blocked by other ASEAN members. When the Philippines first proposed phasing out tariffs to achieve greater economic cooperation through a CU in 1987, this was rebuffed by Indonesia which did not want a timeline to be attached to the proposal.

But the 1980s witnessed significant change in the region. Japan was seeking investment to neighboring countries in the region after the 1985 Plaza Accord forced the value of the yen higher in the hope that this would narrow its trade surpluses with countries like the US and UK. Government officials of ASEAN realized that formalizing regionalization could attract such investment and minimize investment diversion to China (Bowles and MacLean, 1993). When Thailand proposed an AFTA five years later in 1992, the six ASEAN states were ready to adopt the proposal through the AFTA Framework Agreement. In the Agreement, the members decided to implement a free trade area in 2008. This would be achieved through the Common Effective Preferential Tariff (CEPT) Scheme that would eliminate tariffs on all manufactured products among members in phases. Tariffs on products that were in the CEPT Scheme would be reduced to 0–5% by 2008. Those products with tariffs over 20% would be given another five to eight years for reduction to 20%. The final phase would see these tariffs on these products further reduced to 0–5% within seven years. However, the 2008 dateline for establishing AFTA was subsequently brought forward to 2002 as countries like Singapore had gone ahead and removed many import tariffs by the late 1990s.

Notwithstanding the implementation of AFTA, Southeast Asian regionalism is a local model that does not attempt to replicate either the EU or NAFTA (Acharya, 2004). By this, it is meant that states in ASEAN adapted local institutions to international norms. Called the "ASEAN way", these norms reflect political elites' construction of a regional identity consistent with local cultural values. Malaysia, for example, began to promote "Asian values" as a way to exclude western countries from ASEAN regionalism in the 1990s because they were perceived to be culturally different. Asian values generally favor consensus-building and group harmony when state officials interact with one another. They view American style communications as blunt and adversarial with little regard for social harmony. By making consensus-building and social harmony a priority, coming to mutual agreements on trade among many members has not been easy. Such values also create barriers for the establishment of an FTA with non-Asian countries such as the United States. Until recently, the Asia Pacific Economic Forum (APEC) was the closest to a trans-Pacific regional arrangement. But APEC appears to function as a forum rather than a serious regional trade arrangement. This is because Asian countries are highly sensitive to any overture that would suggest the overreach of a foreign authority. Three of the main principles defining ASEAN clearly articulate the countries' desire for protection of domestic sovereignty. They are: (i) mutual respect for the independence, sovereignty, equality, territorial integrity and national identity of all nations; (ii) the right of every state to lead its national existence free from external interference, subversion or coercion; and (iii) non-interference in the internal affairs of one another (www.ASEAN.org). Given these principles, it is difficult to envision the countries embracing a supranational institution that would seek regional rather than local or national coordination of economic policies.

Despite these obstacles, twelve APEC members have moved ahead to form a free trade area. The US is currently negotiating the Trans-Pacific Partnership (TPP) with eleven countries (Australia, Brunei, Canada, Chile, Japan, Malaysia, Mexico, New Zealand, Peru, Singapore and Vietnam) to advance an FTA. Considered to be a blueprint for FTA agreements in the future because of its broader coverage of issues, TPP seeks to liberalize trade, investment and services in the region with the goal of forming a free trade area of the Asia-Pacific (FTAPP). Among Asian countries, TPP is also an instrument for integrating regional production networks. While only twelve countries are currently involved in the negotiation, the plan is to gradually extend the free trade area to countries around the region including South Korea and China. Unlike other regional trade agreements, the FTAPP is a transcontinental regional trade pact that captures both regional and transnational linkages, reflecting new patterns of regionalization in a globalizing world.

However, President Obama faces considerable criticism from members of his own party because of concerns that the pact does not sufficiently protect worker rights and the environment. Contestation of the TPP is consistent with earlier discussion on the cultural divide across the Pacific between Asian countries which prefer to develop trade deals that leave out political considerations, in contrast to the United States where labor and environmental groups seek active participation in such deals. Not surprising, the divide has Asian diplomats frustrated by what they perceived to be a lack of US engagement with the region. Inclusion of the US in the trade pact is also a question of geography. Long a major market for many of the countries here, such a pact would transform the nature of regional ties by integrating economies across the Pacific where flows of people, not just goods and services, are considerable. In response to the lack of enthusiasm by US Congress, Singapore's foreign minister K. Shanmugan asked: "Do you want to be part of the region, or do you want to be out of the region?" (cited in Soble, 2015). While the TPP is unlikely to move forward given the 2016 US presidential election outcome, the aforementioned question implies that the US is regarded to be an outsider despite its geographical location in the Pacific. For the Asian countries, being part of the region is predominantly economic, requiring investment in trade and the market rather than in cultural relationships.

MERCOSUR

In 1991, four South American countries, Argentina, Brazil, Paraguay and Uruguay, signed the Treaty of Asuncion to achieve freer trade. The Treaty's goal was to establish the Common Market of the South, also known as MERCOSUR. For many observers, this was an important step towards economic integration in the region where previous initiatives had failed. Historical rivalry between Argentina and Brazil to dominate the South American continent has now been transformed into possibilities for cooperation. More importantly, MERCOSUR members have moved ahead with a CU, which is beyond what NAFTA and AFTA have done because a CU represents a higher stage of economic integration. Since then, the regional group has expanded its size and is in the process of admitting another member, Venezuela. The entry of Venezuela created some problems because the socialist leaning country is suspicious about free trade, but its endowment of oil is attractive to MERCOSUR's larger members. Paraguay had opposed Venezuela's membership, but it has in turn been suspended as a member because the remaining three partners were against Paraguay's 2012 impeachment of its president, Fernando Lugo.

Like its Southeast Asian counterparts, intra-regional trade was quite low when MERCOSUR was formed. Table 4.2 shows that the share of intra-regional trade among the five members was around 7.6% in 1990. This increased to 13.6% in 2013, though the years from 1998 to 2003 also saw a drop in intra-regional exports as members encountered an economic crisis. Brazil devalued its currency in 1999 after suffering years of budget deficits, while Argentina experienced a debt crisis in 2001 and had to be bailed out by the International Monetary Fund. From 2003 onwards, intra-regional trade expanded significantly. However, economic integration remains a challenge. Many of the countries are commodity-rich (agricultural and mineral products) but the market for commodities tends to be non-members. As new institutional theory predicts, MERCOSUR is made up of many working groups and committees working together to foster learning and policy-making. But institutional mechanisms for resolving disputes remain weak and larger member nations can disadvantage smaller members through unilateral acts.

Overall, MERCOSUR is one of very few regional pacts among developing countries that harbors goals of greater economic integration beyond an FTA. However, it has also been criticized for a low level of institutionalization which makes coordination of economic policies difficult. This is because members here share ASEAN's concern for sovereignty, favoring consensus over hard rules (Pena and Rozemberg, 2005). Both AFTA and MERCOSUR demonstrate the difficulties of adopting a western model of institutional integration that assumes legal interactions should be an important goal of regionalism.

SUMMARY

International trade is increasingly a governed process. Firms remain important actors in the buying and selling of goods and services that underscore world trade circulation. But states, civic groups and stakeholders have important roles to play that influence trade's impacts on local and national economic development as well as citizens' lives. Much of this governance is geared towards ensuring that trade remains as free as possible. But bottom-up participation from citizens, labor and environmental groups has also transformed the character of governance resulting in greater appreciation of differences in goals, identity, negative spillovers and geopolitics. Much of trade governance has occurred at the continental regional scale, but the WTO represents the most ambitious governing mechanism for ensuring global free trade.

The major points of this chapter may be summarized as follows:

- Regions have become the most popular scale of organizing international trade. Common borders or spatial proximity enhance the exploitation of regional economies of scale through their influence on markets, geopolitics and institutions.
- Three major theories explain regionalization and regionalism tendencies. They are neoliberalism, neofunctionalism and constructivism. All three theories generally agree that increased regionalism must be accompanied by a process of institution-building, but they differ on how the objectives and means of institutionalism are to be achieved.
- The WTO was born in 1995, taking over from its predecessor GATT, and endowed with greater legal authority to handle trade disputes. Trade agreements have expanded to include issues of trade and labor, trade and environment, and intellectual property.
- The most advanced expression of regionalism is the EU, which has achieved monetary union. However, scaling up loyalties has proved to be difficult as citizens balk from time to time at transaction cost efficiency as a major factor determining EU integration.
- Most regionalism efforts have remained at the lowest level of integration, namely the free trade area. The NAFTA along with the AFTA are two such examples. Both were implemented with mixed results. For example, intra-regional trade within AFTA remains relatively low at around one-quarter of total trade.
- MERCOSUR has achieved higher integration than either NAFTA or AFTA with a CU. Specialization in primary products, however, has kept intra-regional trade fairly low.

SUGGESTED READING

The literature on trade governance can get very technical, particularly with respect to WTO rules, regulations, agreements and legal language. Organizations like the WTO, EU and ASEAN host websites (see resources below) that summarize the structure of their governance. For more details, you may refer to the following books.

Hinkelman, E.G. (2005) *Dictionary of International Trade*. Novata, CA: World Trade Press.
For a quick preview of various trade terms and concepts, check out this dictionary. It serves as a good reference book.
McCormick, J. (2014) *Understanding the European Union: A Concise Introduction*. Basingstoke: Palgrave-MacMillan, 6th edition.
The suggested readings offer an interdisciplinary view of trade governance. McCormick's book is designed for those with little background on the subject matter. Soo's book is more critical, documenting the opposition against trade governance.
Soo, Y.K. (2010) *Power and the Governance of Global Trade: From GATT to WTO*. Ithaca: Cornell University Press.

RESOURCES

There are several sources that publish statistics on international trade. These include the International Monetary Fund, United Nations and the European Union. Many of the statistics may be downloaded from the Internet but more detailed data will need to be purchased.

Statistical sources

- The International Monetary Fund compiles economic and financial data including trade data for individual countries.
- International Monetary Fund (IMF) *International Financial Statistics*, Washington DC. Statistics on exports, imports, exchange rate, current accounts. The statistics are published monthly and annually.
- International Monetary Fund (IMF) *Direction of Trade Statistics Yearbook*, Washington, DC.

Web resources

- The following websites provide information on the history, structure and evolution of various supra- and world organizations. They are also good sources of trade statistics.

- World Trade Organization (WTO): www.wto.org
- European Union (EU): europa.eu
- North American Free Trade Agreement (NAFTA): www.naftanow.org
- ASEAN Free Trade Agreement: Asean.org
- MERCOSUR: www.mercosur.int (Spanish or Portuguese only)

5

TRADE AND DEVELOPMENT

China's trade relationship with Europe and the United States has attracted widespread media coverage. The British Broadcasting Corporation announced that China would surpass the US as the world's largest trading country (*BBC*, 2014) although its export growth has since slowed down. China's high export growth has come at a price: the country has a huge trade surplus with Europe and the US, and this is creating trade conflicts. Twenty years earlier, it was Japan that was regarded as the "rogue" country. Like China, its trade with the West was highly unbalanced: Europe and the US in particular experienced severe trade deficits with Japan in the 1980s and 1990s. What do China, Japan and nineteenth-century Britain have in common? The answer is that their growth has been led by trade, and they export more than they import. The notion that a country's wealth depends on a trade surplus is often referred to as mercantilism and may be traced to Britain's accumulation of gold through exports in the sixteenth to eighteenth centuries. Ascent of Britain during this period is associated with gross domestic product (GDP) and export growth rates that were well above those of the previous two centuries. At the height of its trade empire in 1870, Britain led Europe in per capita GDP ($3,191) followed by the Netherlands ($2,753) and Belgium ($2,697) (Maddison, 2006: Table B-21). At this time Japan was still quite poor, trailing Europe with a GDP per capita of only $737, and characterized by a standard of living that was only slightly higher than that of China or India. However, this pattern was reversed during the second half of the twentieth century. In 1998, Japan's income level had risen to $20,413 while Britain's had stagnated at around $18,714. That Japan had become the fourth richest nation is in part explained by the country's flood of exports on the international market as firms like Toyota and Sony made their mark, impressing consumers with high quality manufacturing goods.

Emulating Japan, East and Southeast Asia also began to pursue a model of exports that the World Bank (1993) has called "The East Asian Miracle". By a miracle, the authors of the report were referring to sustained, often double digit, GDP growth rates over the 1980s and 1990s which they maintained were the result of "getting the basics right" (p. 5). This, in turn, involved following the prescriptions of neoclassical (orthodox) economics and engaging in high saving, high investment and high export growth (p. 8). Today, Japan's export model, sometimes referred to as the "flying geese model", continues to be replicated across parts of Asia as China joins its neighbors and renders exports a central industrial strategy in modernizing its economy. The flying geese model is a metaphor for describing changing comparative advantage among countries in East Asia. It illustrates a sequential industrial take-off that happens when a certain country has reached a significant share of manufactured exports (Fujita et al., 2011). China is the latest of the "Asian export geese" and has garnered more attention than most of its forerunners because of the enormous size of its trade surplus with the West.

That countries in the Asia Pacific region have benefited economically from exports is well-documented by the 1993 World Bank report. Yet East Asia's case is by no means readily generalizable to other countries on the periphery such as those in Africa and Latin America. Economic growth and development is a complex issue where trade is only one factor in the equation. More than forty years ago, Kravis (1970) concluded that international trade should be regarded as a "handmaiden" rather than an "engine" of economic growth. The implication is that trade does not always explain why some countries grow rapidly. However, trade does expose firms to international prices and competition. In this sense, it may support economic growth through improving the quality of goods and services and the efficiency of their production (see Chapter 2). Consider the following finding from a recent survey of over 26,000 citizens in the European Union: on average, 28% believe that a priority of the EU's trade policy should be to help developing countries (TNS Opinion & Social, 2010). Citizens from Nordic countries such as

Denmark (37%) and Sweden (44%) are more likely to embrace such a priority than poorer countries like Latvia (14%) and Czech Republic (14%). What the survey suggests is that at least one benefit of international trade might be to positively influence the economic growth and development of poorer countries. But what is the record of trade here? Has it helped developing countries economically? The rest of the chapter will attempt to shed some light on this question.

DYNAMIC COMPARATIVE ADVANTAGE

In order to understand the role of trade in a country's economic growth and development, we first clarify the terms "growth" and "development", which, though related, are not synonymous. On the one hand, economic growth refers to changes in a country's output. This change is typically measured by the country's real or inflation adjusted GDP or GNP (gross national product). Development, on the other hand, is a broader concept that takes into account not only the material well-being of citizens in a country, but also their social and political aspirations. It thus involves a deeper qualitative transformation of society including institutional changes and improvements across multiple dimensions of what the United Nations refers to as the overall quality of life. While it is generally expected that many years of high GDP growth may lead to improved material and social well-being for a country's citizens, the latter may not be realized if that growth is not targeted at these ends. Citizens of low growth countries, for example, can still experience relative well-being if governments and organizations of the country prioritize such a goal. A good case is Bhutan, which, despite being relatively impoverished in a material sense, has a relatively high level of individual well-being. At least we are told that Bhutan is the "happiest" country in the world.

Econometric studies examining the effect of trade on economic growth report somewhat mixed results. Some studies show that the effect of exports is positive (Mijiyawa, 2013; Poon, 1995). Others have found that the export effect is either negative (Kwabena, 1991), or that a threshold of human capital must be reached before exports will positively influence growth (Sheridan, 2014). Notwithstanding the mixed evidence, East Asia's high growth rates in the last twenty to thirty years, reaching double digits at times, are often inextricably linked to an industrialization model that emphasizes exports. One way to explain the pattern of exports among the countries here is to apply Balassa's (1977) dynamic model of comparative advantage. In this model, Balassa regards economic development to be a linear process involving the gradual accumulation of physical capital, skill, human capital, technology and know-how among firms. As accumulation occurs, a country's comparative advantage will also change to reflect relative shifts in factor intensity. This implies that a country will move from producing less skilled products to more skill-intensive products through a process of catch-up. Balassa envisages that the catch-up process will occur in stages as countries acquire initial comparative advantage by first specializing in, and exporting, relatively simple consumer goods. Such exports are usually associated with textiles and apparel. In the next stage, the country embarks on a process of learning by substituting imports with domestic production. Once the country has mastered the production of imports, it should begin exporting them. The model thus intertwines import-substitution with export-orientation in various stages that enable the country to gradually acquire comparative advantage in more technologically sophisticated goods.

UNEQUAL EXCHANGE

Balassa's stages of comparative advantage model offers a normative framework to attain economic development through trade. However, years of colonial exploitation of raw materials from African and Latin American countries have also raised suspicions about the benefits of exports among these countries. Such suspicions may be traced to two sources. First, as we discussed in Chapter 2, influential scholars such as Raul Prebisch (1950) and Hans Singer (1987) questioned if those exports, often destined for industrial markets, would benefit peripheral countries in Latin America like they have in the West. They argued that Latin America is heavily dependent on core industrial markets for exports that in turn reinforce patterns of unequal exchange between developing and industrialized countries that began in the colonial era. Since developing countries are endowed with abundant raw materials and cheap labor, the comparative advantage thesis suggests that they should produce and export lower value goods. Such a spatial division of labor, however, unfairly favors the core countries of the West. Industrial catch-up is unlikely to happen because core countries would always be one step ahead in techno-logical sophistication. Second, consider Table 5.1, which shows the principal exports of a sample of African countries. The principal exports of the countries comprise primary commodities including cotton, coffee, cocoa, vegetables, fish, gold, iron ore, and oil from bituminous minerals. The shares of these exports range from 41% to 96%. Concentration of primary exports poses problems for develop-ing countries if the exports are subjected to unstable markets through volatility in prices and deteriorating terms of trade.

As Chapter 2 shows, the terms of trade argument contends that developing countries tend to specialize in primary exports while advanced industrial countries (AICs) specialize in manufactured exports. Primary exports are subject to volatile price fluctuations, and downward relative price trends over the long term work against a developing country's terms of trade. Table 5.1 would appear to support such a thesis since the African countries in question export relatively few manufactured goods. According to UNCTAD (2011b), the primary exports of some ninety-six developing countries in 2008/09 form more than 50% of their overall export basket. If fuels are excluded from the picture, some fifty-eight developing countries are still dependent on primary commodities in their exports. This is not to say that AICs do not export any primary commodities: the EU and US, for instance, are major exporters of wheat and the US is the world's largest maize exporter. Likewise, Australia and Canada are important exporters of minerals but they also export manufactured goods like automobiles and industrial equipment.

In contrast, manufacturing is a fledgling industry among the coun-tries listed in Table 5.1, which are also some of the poorest countries in the world. This structure of exports translates into a pattern of spatial dependency, which on a broader geographical scale may be thought of as a core–periphery pattern where peripheral developing countries are dependent on the core markets of developed countries for their exports. As long as such a structure persists, then developing countries are unlikely to enjoy dynamic comparative advantages over time, leaving them trapped in a cycle of underdevelopment. Primary exports are subjected to declining terms of trade over time. Statistics provided by UNCTAD (2011b) show that agricultural raw material prices show an overall downward trend (in constant US dollars) from

Table 5.1 Principal exports of selected African countries: 2007–13 average share of total exports (%)

	Africa	Rest of the world
Benin	Petroleum, bit minerals* (41.2%)	Cotton, fruits and nuts (57.3%)
Chad	Cotton, yarn, textiles (43.3%)	Petroleum, bit minerals (95.7%)
Cote d'Ivoire	Petroleum, bit minerals (45.6%)	Cocoa, petroleum, bit minerals (63.6%)
Equatorial Guinea	Petroleum, bit minerals (78.8%)	Petroleum, bit minerals (93.3%)
Ethiopia	Vegetables, live animals (67.1%)	Coffee, oil seeds, fruits (54.5%)
Guinea	Fish, coffee (52.1%)	Aluminium, natural gas (66.1%)
Mali	Gold, live animals (86.1%)	Cotton, gold (74.2%)
Mauritania	Fish, gold (81.3%)	Iron ore, copper (65.2%)
Sudan	Petroleum, bit minerals (60.2%)	Petroleum, bit minerals (87.4%)

Source: adapted from UNCTAD (2013b)

Note: * bit mineral refers to bituminous minerals

1960 to 2010. One explanation is that primary commodities may be readily substituted by technology. The case of cotton production illustrates this. Demand for cotton fluctuates and has even fallen because the apparel industry is able to turn to cheaper substitutes such as synthetic fibers to manufacture clothing. Since AICs are more technology- and human capital-intensive, manufactured exports enjoy a higher price because they reflect an innovation rent. Developing countries are unable to capture such rents as long as they are dependent on core countries for their exports, and as long as they continue to specialize in primary exports that require few technological inputs.

Deteriorating terms of trade among developing countries are not a recent phenomenon. As Williamson (2011) has shown in his historical analysis of trade and poverty, when Europe was undergoing its industrial revolution, developing countries were experiencing deindustrialization. In 1750, for instance, India and China were just as industrialized as Western Europe, producing more than half of world manufacturing output. As manufactures in Europe embodied more and more technology, raising the region's productivity, this initiated a process of global spatial divergence that contributed to the present core–periphery pattern of trade. Core countries in the West grew far more rapidly than peripheral developing countries. As growth patterns diverged, so did trade patterns. Western countries began to specialize more and more in manufactured exports while developing countries specialized in primary commodities leading to a pronounced spatial division of labor between core and peripheral regions. In effect, then, developing countries' participation in international trade had the effect of deindustrialization as export specialization meant that the primary sector was favored over manufacturing. Furthermore, Williamson shows that primary exporters have faced greater price volatility than manufacturing exporters, thus supporting Prebisch and Singer's structural explanation that the core–peripheral pattern of trade disadvantages peripheral countries by subjecting them to a secular decline in terms of trade. As some developing nations jump from primary exports to low-technology manufactured exports, particularly apparel, so their fates also have withered as the terms of trade for many low-priced manufactured commodities have deteriorated with the emergence of China.

What are the implications of unfavorable terms of trade? One implication is that following Balassa's stages of comparative advantage model may be quite difficult since developing countries are importing capital goods without the infrastructure and know-how to turn them into manufactures for export. Prebisch and Singer's thesis heavily influenced countries in Latin America in the 1960s. Their solution for changing the export structure and core–periphery relationship was to embark on an industrialization strategy that focused on replacing imports with domestic manufactures. This has often been called the import-substitution industrialization (ISI) model. In contrast, countries in East Asia eschewed the ISI model in favor of export promotion following the lead of Japan. East Asia's export-promotion industrialization (EPI) model has been praised by the World Bank for its positive growth and development outcomes.

IMPORT-SUBSTITUTION AND EXPORT PROMOTION

Historically, economic development in the West has been accompanied by sectoral transformation from primary to manufacturing and then advanced producer services. While such a linear view of development has been challenged, conventional wisdom has it that countries with a higher level of industrialization should also create more wealth. Western Europe and the US are considered to be core countries because manufacturing performance during the nineteenth century produced unprecedented industrial and trade outputs that created "growth miracles" (Williamson, 2011: 22). Developing countries have also been encouraged to initiate their own industrial revolutions. Given the popularity of Prebisch and Singer's trade development theory in the 1950s and 1960s, one way to industrialize for then newly independent developing countries without becoming too dependent on core countries was to embark on an import-substitution model (ISI). Here domestic industries were encouraged to develop through various forms of protectionism, replacing foreign imports with a country's own domestic products. The rationale was to protect domestic industries from more competitive foreign importers and to change the structure of the economy of a developing country (that is, to become industrialized without relying too much on the markets of core countries). Justification for protecting domestic industries under ISI may be traced to the infant industry argument. This framework suggests that new firms and sectors of a developing country will need time to develop capacity and efficiency to compete with foreign firms. The relative lack of efficiency of infant industries is thought to hinge on relatively low levels of technological sophistication, less-skilled workers and lack of knowledge about the market. Tariffs on imports are the preferred mechanism for protecting emerging firms and sectors. Some are critical of these policies suggesting that they encourage rent-seeking behavior with firms chasing subsidies to protect their industry. For this reason, many scholars do not view ISI favorably.

ISI was quite popular among Latin American countries in the 1960s and 1970s. While the goal of import-substitution was to transform the unequal trade relationship between core and peripheral countries that frees the latter from export dependence, it may have contributed to Latin America's lower growth compared to East Asia in the 1980s. In 1870, Latin America and Asia's share of world merchandise exports were 9.7% and 1.7% respectively. This was a time when the Portuguese and Spanish were heavily involved with sugar and cotton trade across the Atlantic. By 1998, however, Asia's share of world merchandise exports had risen to 12.6% while Latin America's share was no higher than one hundred years earlier. If all exports are considered, then Latin America's exports fell from 5.4% to 4.9% while Asia's rose from 13.9% to 27.1% over the same period. The pattern for Africa is similar to Latin America: export shares of world markets fell from 4.6% in 1870 to 2.7% in 1998 (Maddison, 2006: Table 3-2b). The fall in exports cannot be attributed to import–substitution policies alone in both Latin America and Africa, but they may have contributed to the situation. At the height of import–substitution in 1973, Latin America's export share fell to its lowest level (3.9%) before rebounding in 1998. When the export trend is compared to per capita GDP growth, then most of the countries of Latin America experienced negative growth rates between 1980 and 1990 (Maddison, 2006: Table 3-22). One of the key explanations for the failure of ISI policies is that the developing countries did not have strong enough internal markets to support the growth of their own manufactures.

A second way to industrialize through trade is to apply the export–promotion model. According to Bhagwati (1988), this does not mean devising policy tools and instruments that favor exports. Instead, an EPI strategy refers to the removal of any discrimination against exporting. This itself is alleged to be an incentive for firms to export. The term export–promotion is thus compared against protection levels that were rife in the 1960s as a result of countries adopting import–substitution. Recall that under ISI, protectionism is legitimized through the infant industry argument. Export promotion chips away the level of protectionism and restores a more neutral response to exports. In this sense, being export–oriented does not preclude the country from practicing import–substitution. Nor does it preclude the country from being somewhat interventionist since East Asian countries like Japan and South Korea are not as open to foreign direct investment (FDI) compared to their southern neighbor Singapore. Those who support EPI argue that the countries' take-off in capital investment in the 1960s was correlated with their adoption of the model. Exporting abroad in effect removes the constraints of domestic market size resulting in higher investment returns. Table 5.2 compares the share of manufactured exports over total exports for selected Latin America and East and Southeast Asian countries from 1980 to 2013. East Asian economies like Hong Kong,

Singapore and South Korea all display very high shares of over 90% suggesting that the countries were industrializing rapidly by 1980 and exporting goods heavily. Clearly, all three countries are also relatively small so exporting their manufactures is essential in order to overcome the constraints of a limited domestic market. But size does not completely explain the numbers in Table 5.2 since small countries in Latin America like Bolivia, Chile and Paraguay are characterized by low rather than high shares. Similarly, when we compare large countries across the two regions, Indonesia, Brazil and Argentina all exhibit relatively similar manufactured export shares around one-third of total exports. This might be expected because these are resource-rich countries. Mexico, however, balks the pattern. Compared to its neighbors, Mexico embarked on a course of export-promotion in the 1990s, raising its manufactured export share from 12% to 74% between 1980 and 2013. Perhaps the most interesting country is China. Given its sizeable domestic market, its

Table 5.2 Share of manufactured exports (%)

Country	1980	1990	2013
1. Latin America			
Argentina	23	19	32
Bolivia	3	5	5
Brazil	37	52	35
Chile	9	11	14
Colombia	20	25	18
Mexico	12	43	74
Paraguay	12	10	9
Peru	17	18	15
Uruguay	38	39	24
2. East & Southeast Asia			
China	–	72	94
Hong Kong	96	95	69
Indonesia	2	35	36
Japan	95	96	90
Malaysia	19	54	62
Singapore	47	72	70
South Korea	90	94	85

Source: *World Development Report*, various issues

share of manufactured exports of 94% in 2013 is well above what we would expect for a country of this size. Manufactured exports have clearly been a key driver of the country's industrialization.

Overall, EPI has many supporters and is firmly entrenched in World Bank and International Monetary Fund (IMF) policies, often called the Washington Consensus. Exports enable a country to achieve economies of scale when markets are small or do not have the capacity to absorb all domestic production. A small group of authors, however, maintain that ISI has been helpful in propelling developing countries to greater industrialization. Adewale's (2012) study of Brazil and South Africa's ISI, for instance, favors the latter view, arguing that ISI helped both countries transform from agricultural to industrializing economies. Whether one favors ISI or EPI, it is fair to say that most countries apply a mix of both strategies. Historically, countries like Argentina, for example, had been major agricultural exporters. Diversification of exports to the industrial sector occurred at a much slower pace than in East Asia, and transnational corporations were far more interested in exports of resources than manufactured goods. Moreover, imports remain an important mechanism by which a country acquires intermediate goods that it does not yet have the know-how or capability to produce. This also appeared to be the case in East Asia which practiced some level of stages of comparative advantage intertwining ISI and EPI at various periods of time. It is critical to note that in both ISI and EPI policies, the state plays a major role in national growth and development strategy.

BOX 5.1   ISI and Malaysia's automotive industry

In a bid to develop a national industry, the government of Malaysia began to promote heavy industries in the 1980s. Inspired by the Japanese and Korean model of development that had produced national industries, the automobile industry was targeted. This led to the establishment of the first auto manufacturer Proton in 1983. To develop the Proton car, a second round of import-substitution industrialization (ISI) was initiated with the objective of nurturing a domestic automobile sector. This round of ISI was different from that of the 1960s in that the government believed that building a heavy industrial base would deepen the country's industrialization by spawning vertical linkages with domestic suppliers. It meant imposing protection levels including import restrictions for foreign parts and exemption from duty for domestic suppliers. In particular, the government was interested in grooming the native Bumiputra class (a term that refers to native Malays and the indigenous population) which had lagged behind the country's Chinese minority economically. Bumiputra suppliers and vendors were targeted for economic development by increasing their participation in the automotive sector.

Protectionism was high. Tariff levels of between 90% and 200% were imposed in 1982 on completely built up (CBU) passenger cars. Proton also enjoyed exemption from 40% import tariffs on completely knocked-down (CKU) parts. In addition, the company was protected by non-tariff barriers as CBU vehicles and CKU units into Malaysia were restricted. Bumiputra vendors benefited from local content requirement (LCR) policies that limited the ability of local producers to import various parts (e.g. radiator and tire) of a vehicle. However, Malaysia also opened the country to foreign direct investment so that many import-substituting industries involved foreign firms. The Japanese Mitsubishi Corporation and Mitsubishi Motors were invited to be shareholders and to provide technical assistance as well as components to the Proton automaker. This partnership benefited the Japanese companies tremendously. While Proton's competitors were subjected to 40% import duty for importing parts that are necessary for assembly, the car, Proton, on the other hand, was exempted from paying such a duty for Mitsubishi parts.

Proton's record to date has been somewhat mixed. While it has successfully exported cars to the United Kingdom (UK), production costs remain relatively high because of its small domestic market and inability to scale up production. Critics charge that development of the Malay automobile industry has not been accompanied by a deepening of the industrial base through backward and forward linkages since many parts are imported and key technology is in the hands of its Japanese partner (Lim, 2001). Also, because the industry has been developed with considerable assistance from the government, it is less efficient compared to foreign competitors. Writing in the country's news media, Gunasegaram (2010) suggests that the prices of Proton cars are not commensurate with their quality because the automaker has been protected for far too long and has not kept up with technology. This contrasts with South Korea where local, rather than foreign, firms took the lead in creating national champions through import-substitution.

ASIAN FLYING GEESE

Japan: Old goose?

Not everyone agrees that EPI is responsible for East Asia's high growth rates. In a provocative article published shortly after the World Bank's East Asian Miracle report, Krugman (1994) argued that economic growth of these countries was influenced by the mobilization of resources that was not accompanied by productivity or efficiency gains. He maintained that capital investment rather than productivity arising from exports influenced the high growth rates. For instance, the ratio of investment to GDP in 1980 was well over 30% for East Asian economies with Singapore leading at 45%. Other critics began to challenge prevailing orthodoxy as well.

Of the theories seeking to offer an explanation that departs from orthodoxy, the developmental state theory (DST) by Chalmers Johnson (1982) has been the most popular. Johnson offers an institutional explanation of the growth of Asian countries using Japan as his case study. He points to the state's overarching priority in economic development. While there is some degree of the private market operating under his model, the state is assumed to play a key role in reaching the goals of development. The major institutional apparatus by which the state realizes economic development is the government technocracy. Highly educated scholars from the best universities were recruited to join the civil service. Talented elite bureaucrats devised industrial policies, and helped to groom successful industries through consultation and cooperation. Firms were protected from the pressure of the stock market, enabling them to pursue long-term market strategies. Johnson singled out Japan's Ministry of International Trade and Industry (MITI) as a prime example of such cooperation. MITI was given the power to control imports as a way to protect domestic industries. Such protection is reminiscent of the arguments put forward by strategic trade scholars who see import control as an industrial policy strategy to groom national winners like Toyota. Among the assistance it provided, MITI widened industry access to generous credit schemes through establishment of the Japan Development Bank. In a sense, institutional arrangements that supported import control, export subsidies and promotion, that is an interventionist approach, is offered as the reason why the export promotion model worked well in Japan.

Another example of institutional arrangement in Japan is the Sogo Shosha. Historically, the principal agents that were engaged in trade consisted not only of merchants, but also large trading companies such as Britain's East India Company and Japan's Sumitomo and Mitsubishi General Trading Companies. The latter are sometimes called the Soga Shosha. This term refers to firms that engage in the trade of all types of goods and services with any country in the world. When Japan ended its geographical isolation in the mid-1800s, it did so by first opening up its ports. Soga Shoshas emerged to help domestic producers navigate foreign markets. The trading companies imported raw materials, exported Japanese goods and helped to secure technology to support Japan's own industrial revolution. They even provided information on trade law and customs, managing half of Japan's trade up to the early 1990s. Today they continue to import more than they export, acting as strategic suppliers of oil and minerals to keiretsus (UNCTAD, 2004). Yonekura and McKinney (2005) suggest that the Sogo Shoshas should be seen as Japan's early transnational companies. In a sense, they are not that different from the East India Company which was responsible for facilitating trade between Britain, India and China in the eighteenth century, transforming its role over time from a trading company to the world's first transnational corporation (Bowen, 2005). However, the role of Soga Shoshas has diminished over time because twenty-first-century trade has become much more complex involving strategic partnerships between large transnationals, suppliers and their global–regional production networks (Yeung, 2016).

Institutional arrangements are not the only factor that influenced Japan's success in exports. One popular argument in the 1990s was that cultural factors also explained Japan's success in exports. At that time, commentators argued that culturally embedded practices hindered foreign imports that reinforced the country's huge trade surpluses in the 1980s and 1990s. Lawrence (1993) maintained that Japan's post-war growth was the outcome of it being a "different trade regime" from the West. By this, he was referring to the distinct form of inter-firm, inter-corporate networks of Japanese industrial groups (keiretsu). A vertical keiretsu, for example, comprises a major manufacturer with a vertical layer of suppliers. Vertical keiretsus like

Toyota, Nissan or Hitachi tend to rely on Japanese suppliers with whom they have developed a trusting relationship for parts and components, potentially locking out foreign suppliers. Then there are distribution keiretsus where networks of affiliated Japanese wholesalers and retailers are favored outlets for manufacturers' distribution of goods. Lawrence suggested that close ties between manufacturers, suppliers and distributors form a cultural barrier to foreign imports.

While the above insitutional and cultural arrangement may have contributed to Japan's trade surplus with many western industrialized countries, an event also occurred that changed the course of its trade with the rest of the world subsequently. Under the Plaza Accord in 1987, Japan agreed to appreciate its yen against the G-7 countries. The Accord was aimed at reducing the country's trade surplus by making exports to the G-7 countries more expensive and foreign imports from these countries cheaper for Japanese consumers and firms. The economic impact of currency appreciation was significant. Japanese firms began to move factories out of the country to East and Southeast Asia. Malaysia, a favorite destination of Japanese outward investment, became a major export platform for Japanese electronics to other industrialized countries. In turn, the dispersion of Japanese industry within East Asia led to the hollowing out of its manufacturing sector, diminishing the quality of domestic investment. Outward investment can be trade-replacing. In this case, Japanese outward investment began to substitute for domestic production rather than complement manufacturing activities (Cowling and Tomlinson, 2011). The overall impact of such hollowing out, with one-third of electronics manufacturing occuring outside the country, is that Japan entered into a period of deindustrialization that has persisted to this day, although industrial decline has been slower than countries in Western Europe (*The Economist*, 2012). For the first time since the 1980s, Japan registered a trade deficit of $92 billion in August of 2014. Once a leading goose in the region, it is being challenged by industrializing neighbors such as South Korea and China.

Asian mature geese

In the early 1950s, South Korea and Taiwan were relatively poor countries. Their income per capita was lower than African countries like Mozambique (Trindale, 2005). In the course of the next five decades, the two East Asian countries, along with Singapore and Hong Kong, grew rapidly, joining the West in terms of high living standards. Success of the four economies in pulling themselves out of poverty in a relatively short period of time has been the source of much attention. Compared to Brazil and Mexico, these are relatively small countries with South Korea hosting the largest population of 50 million. The other three economies are much smaller in size ranging from 5 to 23 million people. A small domestic market will mean that small countries tend to be more export-dependent and outward-looking. One way of ascertaining the level of export dependency is to calculate the share of exports to GDP as illustrated in Table 5.3. The table shows that the share is lower for larger than smaller countries. China and Mexico display the highest shares in 2013 but they are still lower than those of smaller countries like Belgium, Netherlands, Hong Kong, Malaysia and Singapore. One explanation is that large countries can depend on domestic markets to purchase their manufacturing products. American companies, for example, can enjoy economies of scale because of their large domestic market and are less dependent on the international market for sales. Inspired by East Asia, Mexico liberalized its economy in the 1990s and saw a surge of exports, driven largely by NAFTA and a booming maquiladora sector. Both Hong Kong and Singapore's ratios in 2013 were very high at well over 100%. It is possible for the share to be over 100% because these are small economies that are engaged in considerable entrepot trade relative to domestic production. Entrepot trade involves re-exports without any additional processing or value-added.

Table 5.3 shows that East Asian exporting geese—Hong Kong, Singapore, South Korea—all intensified their exports over time as shown by the rise in the export to GDP ratio over the 1980 to 2013 period. Not surprising, pursuit of EPI has generated favorable trade balances for all three countries with G-7 industrialized countries like Canada, Germany, the US and the UK. This positive trade balance peaked in the 2000s. However, by 2013, Hong Kong and Singapore began to experience a trade deficit with the US in the goods sector (Office of the US Trade Representative, www.ustr.gov). The deficit is explained by imports of technology-intensive commodities such as machinery paralleled by a decrease of labor-intensive exports as the Asian countries joined the ranks of industrialized nations. It is also

Table 5.3 Export dependency of selected countries

Country	Exports/GDP (%)	
	1980	*2013*
Large country:		
Japan	13	15
USA	10	14
China	8	26
Brazil	9	13
Indonesia	34	24
Mexico	11	32
Small country:		
Belgium	54	86
Netherlands	52	88
Hong Kong	89	230
Malaysia	57	82
South Korea	30	54
Singapore	202	191
Thailand	24	74

Source: *World Development Report* and *Direction of Trade Statistics Yearbook*, various issues

worth pointing out that the three countries all experienced significant trade deficits with Japan well into the 2000s. They are not well-endowed in natural resources, and imports of oil, gas and minerals are quite high. But this factor does not explain their trade deficits with Japan alone. Japan's investment in the region also plays a role, though the pattern of deficits appears to have reversed recently as Japan's deindustrialization deepens.

South Korea has enjoyed a trade surplus with most G-7 countries except for Japan for a number of years because its domestic manufacturing sector is relatively strong. South Korea produces world-class quality cars and smartphones from giant conglomerates like Hyundai, Samsung and LG Electronics. The DST suggests that like Japan, Korea also embedded EPI in strategic trade and industrial strategy as early as the 1960s. More than a dozen industrial policy interventions were implemented to encourage exports. These include tariff exemptions on intermediate or capital good imports that function as inputs to export industries, import entitlement certificates which exempted export industries from import restrictions, tax breaks for domestic suppliers whose inputs were used by the export industries, and preferential access to credit for exporters including bank loans. There was even an "export day" that honored top exporters with prizes. The developmental state was realized in other ways besides trade intervention. Public corporations were established to lead the government's export-promotion effort. South Korea's first ships, for instance, were built by such a corporation. An example is the Pohang Iron and Steel Company, currently the world's sixth largest steel maker. The company began as a public corporation with government subsidy, but has transformed itself into a transnational company. The evolution of Korea's industries suggests that EPI unfolded in a stages-of-comparative advantage process, beginning with the textile and garment industry (1970s) to heavy manufacturing such as shipbuilding (1980s), capital goods (1990s) and technology exports today. While the government appears to have backed away from the interventions of the 1970s and 1980s, many would agree that EPI would not have happened without strategic trade and industrial policy that underscored developmental state countries. More recent work suggests that domestic institutional factors emphasized by DST need to be complemented by external factors such as the role of US military trade in fostering regional production networks across the Pacific. Glassman and Choi (2014) show that the US military complex created demand for Korean exports and helped groom Korean chaebols through technology transfer.

For other East Asian exporters like Hong Kong, Taiwan and Singapore, rising labor costs have meant that transnational as well as local companies have decided to relocate their production sites and factories to China and the rest of Southeast Asia where wages are cheaper. In particular, Hong Kong, Taiwan and Singapore companies began to invest in neighboring China and Indonesia, creating regional production networks and trade flows. An example of this is the Taiwanese company, Hon Hai Precision Industries, or Foxconn, which is one of the largest electronics companies in the world. As described in Chapter 1, Foxconn began as an original design manufacturer (ODM). The company provides design engineering and mechanical tooling services to customers such as Apple, Sony and Xbox. Foxconn has significant operations in China: its Shenzhen location functions like a small campus providing its quarter of a million employees with meals, dormitories and sports facilities. It has also expanded into Henan, an interior province, in order to secure cheaper labor. The company's sub-regional trade network within and between provinces is important to the economy of areas where they are located. One report estimates that Foxconn's exports from Henan account for more than half of the province's trade (*China Daily*, 2014). As we outlined in Chapter 3, firms are the primary agents that are responsible for the circulation of components and intermediate goods: these flows are often integrated into the regional and global production networks of transnational companies. One consequence of such integration, however, is that the state's ability to design industrial policies as it has done in the past is diminishing. Instead, contracting firms which perform specialized tasks in these countries can simply insert themselves into global production networks facilitating growth of export-based industries through technological upgrading. For this reason, the relevance of the developmental state in sustaining future economic development has been called into question (Yeung, 2016).

China: Soaring or faltering goose?

The entry of China to the World Trade Organization in 2001 is closely associated with its industrialization. Since opening up to the world in 1978, China quickly emerged to capture most of the FDI to developing countries. It has recently surpassed the US to become the world's largest recipient of FDI (Forbes, 2012). From the start, China embarked on a course of industrialization. Unlike many developing countries, a heavy industrial base was already in place—a legacy of the country's socialist era. A significant share of these industries was nationalized and owned by the state although some private capital was still present under socialist China. For example, a British company controlled one woolen mill right up to the late 1950s. However, trade in the 1960s suffered considerably from a US-imposed embargo arising from the Cold War. China's foreign assets abroad were controlled and Chinese transportation curtailed (Bramall, 2009). This changed when the country opened itself to international trade and FDI through market socialism. China's economic growth was so rapid that it soon overtook Japan and the Asian dragons to become the world's largest trading nation today. Indeed, China is widely recognized as the world's largest export factory, churning out billions of dollars' worth of footwear, textiles, garments and toys each year that travel along global production networks to be sold on the shelves of large retail chains like Walmart and Toys "R" Us. Transformation of the industrial and export structure (see Table 5.2) has been paralleled by double digit growth rates for over twenty years, lifting some 680 million people out of extreme poverty (defined here as living on less than $1.25 a day).

Internationally, China's integration with the world economy has significantly affected prevailing trade relationships and geographical patterns. Once a target of criticism for their industrial and mercantilist policies, Japan and its dragons are no longer the center of attention. Rather, as Chapter 1 suggests, that focus has been redirected to China as the EU and the US are now concerned about China's trade imbalance with them. Trade deficits between these countries and China appear to be widening over time, and they are also much larger in size than the deficits accumulated with China's Asian predecessors. Table 5.4 shows the exports and imports of China. In 1990, all G-7 industrialized countries along with Indonesia, Malaysia and South America enjoyed a trade surplus with China. However, over the next twenty years this trend was reversed. Only Japan, Germany, Malaysia and South America continued to enjoy a trade surplus with China in 2013. Interestingly, countries in Sub-Saharan Africa and the Middle East have transformed their relationship from one of deficit to one of surplus. Overall the table points to three implications. First, Germany is China's most important trade partner in Europe. Nearly half of EU exports to China originate from Germany, led by companies like Volkswagen and BASF. China has turned to Germany for goods such as machinery, viewing the trade relationship to be less ideologically driven than its relationship with the US. Second, intra-regional trade in East and Southeast Asia now forms nearly half of the region's overall trade. Geographically, this means that countries in the region are trading more with one another and particularly with China. For instance, China is now Japan's largest trading partner. Only ten years ago, the US was Japan's largest trading partner. Indeed, China has become the largest or second largest trading partner for many countries in East and Southeast Asia. Increased intra-regional trade is a significant development given the region's heavy dependence on core western markets in the past.

Table 5.4 China's exports to and imports from selected countries, 1980–2013 (US$10,000)

G-7 countries	1990		2000		2013	
	Export	Import	Export	Import	Export	Import
Canada	42,963	145,505	315,784	375,108	2,921,672	2,523,697
France	64,609	162,548	371,589	395,125	2,694,847	2,311,929
Germany	185,644	266,347	927,779	1,040,873	6,734,250	9,415,675
Italy	83,515	105,336	380,202	307,843	2,575,266	1,757,381
Japan	901,098	758,712	4,165,431	4,150,968	15,013,259	16,224,557
UK	64,303	137,943	631,010	359,247	5,094,213	1,907,879
USA	517,533	657,090	5,215,643	2,234,757	36,906,386	15,339,486
East & South Asia						
Indonesia	37,902	80,322	306,182	440,195	3,693,049	3,142,428
Malaysia	34,076	84,228	256,487	548,000	4,593,060	6,015,318
Philippines	21,010	8,502	146,441	167,732	1,986,813	1,818,183
Singapore	197,458	84,078	576,104	505,963	4,583,186	3,006,451
South Korea	125,953	68,397	1,129,236	2,320,741	9,116,495	18,307,292
Thailand	79,362	37,099	224,325	438,079	3,271,790	3,852,268
Vietnam	386	337	153,726	92,915	4,858,630	1,689,190
Other developing areas						
South America	25,614	108,630	360,341	477,874	8,434,336	10,986,835
SSA*	39,661	29,568	360,216	534,127	7,081,978	11,069,114
Middle East	126,329	52,099	820,140	1,021,610	11,901,163	16,290,979

Source: UN Comtrade

Note: * Sub-Saharan Africa

Third, a triadic pattern of trade has begun to emerge with China importing raw materials from resource-rich developing countries, and exporting intermediate and consumer goods to more developed countries. This explains its trade deficit with developing countries outside of Asia. Trade data obtained from the China Custom Statistics indicate that three of its top five imports in 2013 were resource-based exports from Africa, the Middle East and South America including plastics, crude petroleum oil and iron ore. Indeed, China has poured FDI into Africa and Latin America, tapping into the mineral wealth of these regions. Despite these changes, China's top exports are all manufactures that target richer countries including automatic data processing machines and units, radio telephone sets, textiles and garments, steel products and furniture.

How did manufacturing so quickly come to dominate China's exports? From the previous section, one explanation is that China has successfully linked its firms to the global commodity chains of foreign companies by wooing FDI to the country. Another explanation lies in its industrial policies. In the eyes of free trade enthusiasts, industrial policy raises the specter of protectionism since it is designed to protect certain industries in order to nurture national industries that are internationally competitive. Google's CEO Eric Schmidt, however, believes that countries in the West need to adopt a model of industrial policy like Japan, South Korea and China in order to lead the next wave of industrialization such as nanotechnology. His call is supported by academic writings that may be traced back to the 1990s. Laura Tyson (1992), a Berkeley professor who served as President Bill Clinton's economic advisor in 1995, believed that principles of comparative advantage do not apply to technology-intensive sectors because they are characterized by high barriers to entry, scale economies and knowledge spillovers which make it difficult to apply free trade's rules of competition (see also 'New Trade Theory' in Chapter 2). She argues that countries should adopt a strategic trade policy that would enable them to "manage" trade. Trade may be managed through trade agreements, fixed quantities, import targets or limited market access (p. 133). The latter would imply some form of protectionism as discussed in Chapter 4.

While the call for managed trade has diminished today, nonetheless, China remains the world's greatest target of anti-dumping actions, suggesting that managed trade remains rife (see Box 5.2).

One reason is that competition in technology between China and the West has intensified and this is most apparent in China's national industries such as the automobile and solar energy sectors. The Chinese government identified large state-owned enterprises to lead the way in building internationally competitive industries. Its leadership in solar panels, however, has been achieved with significant government subsidy, a point we will elaborate further in Chapter 7. Hence the EU has slapped an import tariff of 42% on Chinese solar glass panels while the US has imposed 18% to 35% tariffs on Chinese solar panels using certain components. Protection of its technology sectors is not the only factor dictating trade tensions. China has also been accused of weakening the value of its currency, the Chinese renminbi, a situation often described as "currency war". Here the value of a currency is kept low in order to encourage exports and discourage imports. In response to pressure to appreciate its currency, the renminbi was allowed to fall in value in 2012, but this did not significantly alter trade imbalances between China and countries like the US. One reason is that in a globally integrated world of production networks, what constitutes an "American" or "Chinese" product is not so neatly divided geographically. Take the case of Acura automobiles produced by the Japanese firm Honda. Approximately 65% of Acura cars contain American parts. In contrast, only about 30% of the American Ford Fusion car parts are made in the US. Hence the "Made in China" label does not adequately capture the whole story of Chinese exports since a high proportion of these exports are manufactured by foreign companies (Pan, 2009).

Perhaps because it has industrialized and grown so rapidly, China has displaced previous leading economies of Asia and altered trading patterns within the region and between Asia and the West. China's emergence has influenced the nature of economic competition and geopolitical alliances among Asian countries. For example, its proposed Free Trade Area of the Asia Pacific (FTAAP) competes with the US-led Trans Pacific Partnership or TPP (see Chapter 4). TPP currently excludes China while the FTAAP seeks to broaden membership with China reinstating the ASEAN style of non-interference in governing regional trade (*Channel NewsAsia*, 2014). Yet it should not be forgotten that China's volume of trade is driven by a few provinces reflecting the geographical concentration of FDI and port infrastructure along eastern coastal provinces and cities.

Moreover, a significant number of Chinese citizens remain poor, especially those located inland, away from the more industrialized eastern coast. Bureaucratic competence in poverty alleviation through exports may have led some to call China a developmental state, but such a model should be cautiously applied here: China's bureaucratic capacity remains spatially fragmented and it is implemented at the local level compared to the national competency of bureaucrats in Japan and South Korea (Nolan, 2002). Moreover, exports have been falling since 2015, suggesting that China's growth model may be running out of steam.

Nonetheless, the emergence of China as a major player in the international trading system has resulted in geographical adjustments among other Asian countries. Both the US and EU remain important destinations for the exports of countries in East and Southeast Asia. However, mercantilist-like practices have also diminished among the mature Asian economies. For example, the US census statistics indicate that Hong Kong and Singapore had begun to increase their imports from the US by the late 1990s. Since then, they have been experiencing a trade deficit with the US, importing significant volumes of machinery, electrical machinery, precious stones/metals, aircraft and medical instruments. At the same time, the Japan–US trade surplus has been reduced dramatically by 41% from over $41,104 million (1990) to $24,192 million (2014). Conversely, China's trade surplus with the US has increased ten-fold over this period to $108,860 million. Likewise, according to the European Commission, while the EU has a trade surplus with the US, its 2014 trade deficit with China is larger than that of the US: that is, $137,849 million if all twenty-eight countries are included. China's trade surpluses with industrialized and industrializing countries are accompanied by large inflows of FDI. This has transformed the country into the world's largest recipient of FDI, and the world's largest exporter of manufactured goods, thus earning the label of the world's largest factory.

BOX 5.2   The managed trade of steel

On 19 May 2014, Attorney-General Eric Holder announced that the United States was pursuing the indictment of five members of China's People's Liberation Army for engaging in trade tactics that he believed had bordered on economic espionage. Alleged tactics involved hacking into the computer networks of American companies including US Steel and the US Steelworkers Union. Among the charges, the individuals were alleged to have stolen thousands of emails that provided Chinese companies with information on US Steel's technology and negotiation techniques.

Once a relatively insignificant producer of steel, China has now become the world's top steel producer, overtaking Japan and South Korea, which were major producers in the 1970s and 1980s. China is now responsible for half of the world's steel output. Steel is not only a raw material in the manufacture of many industrial products; most buildings and physical infrastructure (e.g. bridges) require steel to support them. As a newly industrializing economy, steel is a major input in many of China's industries including construction. Much of China's steel is imported from Australia. However, the country has been aggressively scouting for new sources including West Africa, Canada and the United States. In 2010, China's Anshan Iron and Steel Group Corporation decided to invest in five small steel mills in the US with the objective of acquiring electric furnace technology. Hitherto, China's steel industry has been using the blast furnace and basic oxygen furnace to manufacture its steel. The electric furnace technology is more energy efficient than the blast furnace that is also more expensive to maintain. The investment sparked an outcry from the US steel industry, which claimed that China has been practicing unfair trade through export controls. Such controls were aimed at preventing foreign competition in order to protect its domestic steel industry.

The steel trade has been characterized by considerable controversy for the past thirty years. Since the 1990s, US steel companies have engaged in anti-dumping measures to restrict steel imports, campaigning tirelessly to the American public to "stand up for steel". Anti-dumping measures were preceded by voluntary export restraints in the 1960s when Japan and Europe sought to de-escalate the trade conflict by voluntarily agreeing to import quotas with the US. East Asian countries were often targeted because, by then, they had become significant exporters of steel to the US. *The Economist* (1999) reported that the US steel industry had in that decade launched some twenty anti-dumping and ten anti-subsidy actions against eighteen countries that resulted in import tariffs. A major contention of the US steel industry is that Asian governments practice industrial policy that enables their steel industries to export to the US at a lower price. The steel trade regime appears to contradict the principles of free trade because it has been under some form of managed trade for many years (Yoshimatsu, 2003). Yet some scholars believe that managed trade may be justified when foreign competitors' production is being subsidized. The steel trade, in particular, gets the attention of US Congress and presidents because it is a vital industry in the American manufacturing heartland, serving as a reliable domestic supplier to national industries and providing many jobs to residents of the northeastern region of the country.

More recently, the steel trade conflict has shifted to China. Just as steel was vital to the US manufacturing sector in the twentieth century, it is also a strategic industry in China today. Not surprisingly, the government is eager to nurture the industry domestically, raising the ire of US steel exporters. Whereas the US steel industry previously used its domestic institutions such as the Department of Commerce and the International Trade Commission to lodge complaints about unfair trade practices, it turned to the World Trade Organization (WTO) to take up its case against China. The US accused China of imposing countervailing duties and anti-dumping duties on its high-tech steel exports. China imposed these measures after claiming that US exports were undercutting its own domestic manufacturers with low prices. In the case of high-tech grain-oriented flat-rolled electrical steel, used generally for making high-efficiency transformers and electric generators, the WTO ruled in favor of the US. Details of the dispute may be found on the WTO website. From the US point of view, international organizations such as the WTO have provided a mechanism to resolve trade conflicts in a formal and expedient manner. But from China's viewpoint, the WTO's legal practices are too complex for developing countries as they are still learning the legal language. Nonetheless, the steel trade demonstrates that trade does not occur in an institutional vacuum, and may be "managed" strategically among national economies.

SUMMARY

In this chapter, we have highlighted the complex relationship of trade and economic development. Major points of this relationship are as follows:

- Conventional wisdom suggests that developing countries should upgrade the technological inputs of their trade products in stages through dynamic comparative advantage.

- Dynamic comparative advantage is rejected by Latin America scholars because they regard the theory to be static, creating unfavorable terms of trade that perpetuate core–periphery patterns of trade.
- Unfavorable terms of trade encouraged import-substitution among countries in Latin America because this could potentially contribute to the nations' technological upgrading. Such an industrialization strategy tends to be supported by protectionist policies.
- East and Southeast Asian countries turned to export-promotion strategies to industrialize. Their mercantilist-like practices through weak currencies have contributed to trade surpluses with many countries in the West.
- Japan, South Korea, Taiwan and Singapore's export promotion is supported by industrial policies, technocracy and inter-firm alliances that collectively were first described in the DST. The rise of global production networks has rendered the theory less relevant today.
- China has emerged as the world's largest factory, and enjoys trade surpluses with many countries in Asia and the West. It has expanded its trade with Africa and Latin America to source for raw materials.

SUGGESTED READING

CEPAL (2014). *Global Value Chains and World Trade: Prospects and Challenges for Latin America*. Economic Commission for Latin America and the Caribbean (Cepal.org).
This report attempts to clarify global value chains and how Latin American countries might participate in them. It focuses on the agricultural sector and explores how smallholders can play a role in such trade.
Wallerstein, I. (2004) *World Systems Analysis: An Introduction*. Durham, NC: Duke University Press.
This highly readable book traces the historical foundation of core–periphery, crediting its intellectual origin to scholars from developing nations. Connecting core–periphery to a framework that sees the capitalist process as occurring within the larger structure of the world system, it shows how trade is related to the spatial structure of production.
Yeung, H.W.C. (2016) *Strategic Coupling: East Asian Industrial Transformation in The New Global Economy*. Ithaca: Cornell University Press.

Strategic Coupling offers a critique and rethinking of the developmental state. The author argues that as East Asian firms become more integrated into global production networks, so the state's role has diminished considerably in determining trade outcomes.

RESOURCES

Most of the data for this chapter may be found in:

- Asian Development Bank, *Key Indicators for Asia and the Pacific* (Adb.org).
- Comtrade, United Nations (Comtrade.un.org).
- International Monetary Fund (IMF) *International Financial Statistics*. Washington DC. Statistics on exports, imports, exchange rate, current accounts. The statistics are published monthly and annually.
- International Monetary Fund (IMF) *Direction of Trade Statistics Yearbook*. Washington, DC.
- United Nations Conference on Trade and Development (UNCTAD.org).
- World Bank, World Development Indicators.
- World Trade Organization (WTO): www.stat.wto.org

6

IMPACT OF TRADE

In September of 2011, *The Economist* featured an article titled "Multinationals, it turns out, are evil after all". The writer was referring to an oil spill at Bohai Gulf in Northeastern China by the American energy company, ConocoPhillips. Although the state-owned enterprise China National Offshore Oil Company (CNOOC) owned some 51% of the joint venture between the two companies, ConocoPhillips was heavily criticized for spilling some 3,200 barrels of oil into the sea. The oil spill in China is not the first environmental disaster that has happened in the past two decades. One year before the Bohai Gulf spill, an oil rig manned by a drilling operator for British Petroleum sank following an explosion in the Gulf of Mexico. This was followed by three months of oil leaks from the company's pipelines pouring nearly 5 million barrels of oil into the ocean.

Negative environmental impacts are not the only fallout from transnational companies that are principal agents of trade. In Bangladesh, two separate fires in 2012 and 2013 resulted in the deaths of more than 1,000, mostly female, garment workers. Many of the workers were involved in producing apparel for companies like Gap, Tommy Hilfiger and Walmart. Environmental and labor activists maintain that in their search for lower wages and natural resources, transnational corporations' (TNCs') global production networks create unsafe working conditions and negative environmental externalities by their activities. But not all citizens, workers or organizations lose from the trade activities of TNCs. Indeed there are winners as well. In Chapter 2, we explored a series of trade models that showed trade generates benefits as well as costs to consumers and firms alike. In Chapter 5, we showed that exports have contributed to the growth and development of countries in East Asia, The question of who wins and who loses from trade is complex. This chapter outlines a series of impacts of trade on countries and on individual groups of consumers, workers and firms, leaving judgment of the net benefits of trade ultimately to the reader.

SPECIAL ECONOMIC ZONES

Earlier in Chapter 5, we saw that China transformed itself into a leading exporter of garments, toys and footwear. Much of the low-end man- ufacturing of these goods is undertaken in a few geographical locations called special economic zones or SEZs. As firms outsource or interna- tionalize their production, such areas will try to integrate themselves into the global value chains of transnational firms by participating in labor-intensive production segments of the firms' supply networks.

Governments will often set up SEZs to promote trade and foreign direct investment (FDI). SEZs are known by different names depend- ing on the spatial extent of the zone, the custom regime and the nature of regional economic policies. The earliest of such zones, called free ports, may be traced to entrepot centers such as Macau, Hong Kong and Singapore. These were early sites that were advan- tageously located at the confluence of major trading routes between Europe and Asia in the nineteenth century. Their major role was to import goods, then grade, sort and perform minor manufacturing process on the imports before re-exporting them to another country. Most modern SEZs assume the form of an export processing zone or EPZ. The International Labor Organization (ILO) defines EPZs to be "industrial zones with special incentives set up to attract foreign investors, in which imported materials undergo some degree of processing before being (re)-exported again" (www.ilo.org). They are demarcated from other areas in the country in order to promote a friendly business climate. As such, an EPZ is a special regulatory regime that is designed to facilitate exports. EPZ regulations are usually more liberal than the rest of the country in which they are located, supported by incentives to attract FDI.

The first EPZ is often identified as Shannon, Ireland, and much of the growth of EPZs until the 1970s was concentrated in developed countries. However, by the 1980s globalization of production had become a major economic force as companies accelerated the rate of outsourcing and the configuration of supply and distribution networks across the globe. Developing countries began to participate in firms' global production networks through EPZs so that today more than 3,500 of these zones may be found worldwide, the majority of them in Asia and Latin America. Not all developing countries use the term EPZ to describe these special areas. China prefers to call them SEZs while Mexico and Honduras refer to their EPZs as maquiladora.

Whatever the term, EPZs have become a policy instrument to promote regional development. Indeed, some countries establish EPZs in remote areas to kick-start economic development in distressed areas including Kandla (India), Bataan (Philippines) and Main Free Zone (Costa Rica) (World Bank, 2008). For other areas, EPZs are a means to engage in export-led industrialization. We learned from Chapter 5 that import-substitution policies were popular in many developing countries up to the 1980s. Export promotion began to gain influence by the 1990s. Most developing countries, however, were not yet ready to open their door to world competition. Instead they began to experiment with freer trade through these special areas. In China, SEZs represented small-scale experiments in market liberalization that gradually spread along the coast over time. The turn to export-promotion also changed the objectives of establishing EPZs. More and more, they have become areas to alleviate import bias, create employment, and transfer technology from foreign to domestic firms.

Foreign factories that locate within EPZs tend to be concentrated in specific economic sectors. The most popular are those that produce footwear, garments and small electronic or semiconductor components. Table 6.1 reports the top ten exporters of apparel and electronics in 1990 and 2014. Countries in East and Southeast Asia (South Korea, Indonesia, Malaysia, Singapore and Thailand) dominated apparel exports in 1990. This was also the case for electronics (Japan, South Korea, Singapore, Malaysia and Thailand). However, most of these countries were replaced by China in 2014. China is such a prominent exporter that its apparel and electronic exports of US $173 billion and $571 billion, respectively, are larger than the next top nine exporters combined. For this reason, countries in Asia are concerned about trade-diversion from China. Moreover, much of China's exports in the two sectors are driven by factories that are located in SEZs.

Table 6.1 Top ten exporters of apparel and electronics, 1990 and 2014 (US$10,000)

Country	1990	Country	2014
Germany	6,570	China	173,437
South Korea	5,803	Italy	22,508
Portugal	3,463	Germany	19,511
Thailand	2,664	India	16,538
Turkey	2,631	Turkey	16,270
India	2,211	Spain	12,049
Indonesia	1,628	France	10,580
Singapore	1,564	UK	8,445
Greece	1,490	Belgium	8,373
Malaysia	978	USA	5,258

(a) Electronics

Country	1990 ($mi)	Country	2014 ($mi)
Japan	63,804	China	570,940
Germany	36,525	USA	171,966
South Korea	14,772	Germany	147,934
Singapore	12,881	Japan	104,198
Malaysia	8,521	Mexico	80,024
Canada	5,970	France	44,036
Switzerland	5,431	UK	32,131
Spain	2,717	Thailand	30,735
Thailand	2,681	Italy	29,920
Finland	2,093	Czech Rep.	29,029

Source: UN Comtrade

EPZs have not always benefited their countries. Host government subsidies, physical infrastructure and administrative service provisions have been costly, while tax revenues are foregone since imports are subjected to little or no tariffs. Labor critics, in particular, point to the low wages of workers and the poor conditions of employment and life, more generally. For example, some EPZs are fenced-in industrial areas where workers live and work on the factory grounds. The Hon Hai factory in Shenzhen is really a factory town (Stanwick and Stanwick, 2016). More than 400,000 workers toil behind the factory walls, and live and work in a self-contained area that hosts its own housing, bank, hospital, fire station and television broadcasting. To visualize how China's factory towns work, we suggest that the reader watch the four minute video "Foxconn: An exclusive inside look" on Youtube by ABC News.

In many EPZs, the majority of factory workers are young women. Some scholars argue that work is gendered at EPZs because employers believe that garment and electronic component assembly is more suitably performed by females. In reality, the women are a relatively cheap source of labor since they are less likely to become members of unions, they generally have fewer resources to devote to organization, and they comprise a flexible workforce for firms, easily hired and fired as economic conditions dictate. EPZs highlight the plight of women who work in the global supply chains of foreign firms. The employment practices of firms operating within EPZs have raised many concerns. EPZs are also criticized on other grounds. By virtue of their geographical demarcation, EPZs often operate as protected areas or enclaves, spatially isolated from the rest of the country because TNCs here tend to develop few linkages with domestic firms. One benefit of hosting multinational firms in EPZs is the potential for backward linkages to local firms. When the foreign firm sources inputs or raw materials from local firms in the host country, for instance, this helps build backward linkages between local and foreign firms that foster technological upgrading. Unfortunately, EPZ incentives encourage imports that enter duty-free, and multinationals have few incentives to establish backward linkages with domestic firms. Hence local firms may not benefit much from the presence of the foreign firms and their supply networks.

Nonetheless, EPZs have ballooned in number to over 3,000 widely distributed across many countries. This growth has encouraged some commentators to offer a more optimistic assessment of their role within the global economy. It has been suggested that EPZs play an important role in fueling exports from developing countries. While recent figures are not available, cost–benefit analyses indicate that in some countries, they have contributed significantly to employment, FDI and foreign exchange earnings (Sawkut et al., 2009). *The Guardian*, a British newspaper, best sums up the advantages and disadvantages of EPZs in a 2012 headline entitled "Are export processing zones the new sweatshops, or drivers of development?". Visiting a Korean footwear factory in Chittagong, Bangladesh, the writer John Vidal narrates a familiar story: factories that are composed largely of female workers who manufacture millions of shoes a year and make about $1.50 a day. Yet he also acknowledges that significant foreign exchange earnings are being generated from the $1.6 billion worth of exports that are being produced in the country's EPZs. Regardless of where one stands, EPZs are here to stay as more and more developing countries turn to export-promotion as an industrial strategy.

IMPACT ON LABOR

In 1999 delegates to the World Trade Organization (WTO) Ministerial Conference in Seattle gathered to launch a new round of international trade negotiations. The negotiations collapsed and were quickly overshadowed by throngs of anti-globalization protesters. The so-called "Battle of Seattle" brought together a loose coalition of protest groups, united in their opposition to the activities of TNCs and a perceived "race to the bottom", a race to lower labor protections, environmental regulations and consumer protection laws in the name of profit. Street protests of the excesses of global capitalism have continued, more recently appearing in the Occupy Wall Street movement protesting growing wage inequality and policies of austerity that followed the 2008 financial crisis. And, in a 2014 Global Attitudes Survey conducted by the Pew Research Center, only one in five Americans believed that trade creates jobs. Fully 50% of those surveyed in the United States believed that trade largely eliminates jobs and 67% argued that foreign corporations purchasing domestic companies was a bad thing.

In other parts of the world, the reaction to new trade agreements is mixed. Approval of the proposed Transatlantic Trade and Investment Partnership (TTIP) between the United States and the European Union has been delayed and more than three million EU citizens have signed an initiative to block its implementation. A 2007 Oxfam Briefing Paper, *Signing Away the Future*, condemns the rush by richer countries of the world to establish trade and investment agreements with poorer countries, arguing that these agreements undermine the ability of developing countries to implement domestic policies needed to fight poverty. Determining the impacts of trade agreements can be very difficult. The North American Free Trade Agreement (NAFTA) between the US, Canada and Mexico, discussed in Chapter 4, is criticized by many US-based labor groups as responsible for the export of a large number of less-skilled American manufacturing jobs south of the border. While Mexico might have banked on capturing those jobs in the run up to NAFTA's ratification, the job gains did not materialize as expected. What happened? In a word, China! Trade, then, at least as much as it is connected to globalization, has a bad rap. In this section of the chapter, we examine whether this response to trade is justified by exploring the linkages between trade and labor market outcomes in different parts of the world, extending the focus on EPZs outlined above.

TRADE AND LABOR STANDARDS

It is clear that there are significant differences in labor market characteristics around the world. The skill composition of the workforce, wages and conditions of employment vary markedly from one country to the next. These differences reflect levels of development and national income, histories of social and political struggles and the efforts of unions and other institutions to regulate the work environment (Peck, 1996). It is precisely this heterogeneity in labor market conditions that leads many TNCs to fragment operations and distribute components of their value chains to different places where they can access the right skills at the lowest cost. If we imagine the overall cost of labor to reflect not just the wage-level, but conditions of employment including health and safety standards and rights to organize, then an important question to consider is whether globalization and trade have significantly impacted labor standards in developed and less-developed economies. In part, the answer to this question depends upon the nature of work performed in different countries and the extent to which workers in those countries are in competition with one another.

The primary fear within industrialized economies is that increased trade will erode labor standards and conditions of employment that workers and unions have fought for over many decades. This fear is driven by rising competition from emerging economies with lower labor standards. While such competition is generally thought to impact only the bottom-end of the labor market in terms of skills and wages, Rigby and Breau (2008) show that higher levels of education and skill are unlikely to insulate workers in industrialized nations from global competition in the long-run. Emerging economies themselves are not immune to these concerns for two reasons. First, South–South trade competition, or competition between developing economies, is becoming more intense. Second, while less-developed countries recognize that lower labor costs are a key source of competitive advantage, they also understand that to escape the **middle-income trap** they must raise skill-levels and compete for work further up the value added chain. This will require higher wages and better working conditions to induce workers to invest in their own education or **human capital**.

Although there are plenty of horror stories in terms of the abuse of labor by the affiliates of TNCs and more particularly within the factories of external TNC partners in developing economies, what does broader research find in terms of the relationship between labor standards and trade? The evidence for the developing world is mixed. In a recent review paper for the United States International Trade Commission, Salem and Rozental (2012) paint a relatively rosy picture of trade enhancing labor market conditions largely through the movement of workers from informal sector jobs to export-oriented sectors that generally have better labor protection. A more nuanced position is presented by Mosley and Uno (2007) who argue that the impact of globalization and trade on labor rights depends heavily on the way in which countries are integrated into the global economy. Developing a comprehensive data set for middle- and lower-income developing economies, they show that countries attracting substantial flows of FDI tend to experience rising labor standards, while countries that are drawn into the world economy through sub-contracting partnerships of one form or another have generally seen workers' rights eroded, especially those of women. A more balanced assessment overall is offered by Elliott and Freeman (2003).

What about the influence of trade on labor standards in rich countries? Answering this question is difficult because the labor markets of many developed economies have altered so much over the last few decades and many factors have contributed to these changes. What is remarkable is how the nature of work across many developed countries has shifted away from manufacturing toward the service sector over the last half of the twentieth century in a process referred to as **deindustrialization**. In the United States, for example, the manufacturing share of all private sector employment was about 25%

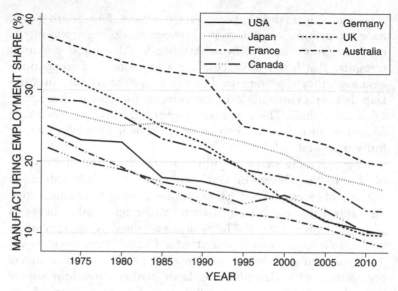

Figure 6.1 Deindustrialization in developed countries

Source: FRED Economic Data, Federal Reserve Bank of St Louis

in 1950, about the same as the services sector overall. By 2000, the manufacturing share of all US employment had fallen to 13%, while the services fraction had increased to more than 60%. This same trend is evident across many advanced, industrialized economies (see Figure 6.1). Accompanying the relative decline of manufacturing jobs, we have seen falling rates of unionization, the growth of part-time over full-time jobs and stagnant wages for many. There is no question that trade and globalization are responsible for some of these changes (see Kletzer, 2002). At the same time, improvements in technology and, at least in the United States, an increase in immigration (both legal and illegal) have also driven changes in the nature of work. Separating the influence of these forces on the labor market is not easy. We return to this question in the next section.

Much of the international community agrees on the need for basic labor protections. The **International Labor Organization** has identified a core set of labor standards (see Box 6.1) adopted by the majority of its members that now total more than 175 countries. A group of eight ILO members, that includes China and the

BOX 6.1 International labor organization

The International Labor Organization (ILO) was formed in 1919 as part of the Treaty of Versailles that ended the First World War. It was tasked with ensuring social justice in the workplace. In 1946, the ILO became a branch of the United Nations. In 1998, the ILO issued its Declaration on Fundamental Rights at Work seeking:

1. Abolition of child labor
2. Elimination of forced or compulsory labor
3. Freedom of association and the right to collective bargaining
4. Elimination of discrimination with respect to employment and occupation

Source: http://www.ilo.org

United States, only recognize two of these standards. (To be fair, US domestic policy provides most of the labor protections outlined in the remaining ILO standards.) How such standards should be implemented is a lot less clear, especially when the discussion shifts to incorporating labor provisions in trade agreements. For developing nations, such requests threaten their fundamental comparative advantage built around cheap labor. They argue that more labor regulation will drive up wages and thus dissuade FDI. There is also suspicion of the motives of advanced, industrialized countries for seeking such labor protections. Do richer nations press for labor standards because they seek the moral high ground, or because they see such standards as a form of protectionist trade policy, allowing them to block exports from parts of the developing world (Burtless, 2001)?

TRADE, JOBS AND WAGES

Richard Freeman provocatively titled a 1995 article, "Are your wages set in Beijing?". He was asking how international trade and the emerging global economy were impacting the wages of low-skilled workers in the United States, Europe and other regions of the industrialized world as competition with low-wage workers in developing economies, like China and India, intensified. There were

Figure 6.2 Timing of increases in wage inequality and trade competition
Source: Atkinson et al., 2011

two good reasons to focus on this issue. First, wage inequality in many industrialized nations accelerated sharply in the late-1970s, at more or less the same time as imports from low-wage countries were beginning to expand. Figure 6.2 should make this link clear, mapping the rise in wage inequality in the United States and the growth of import competition. Second, there is a clear theoretical connection between shifts in relative wages and trade that lies at the core of the Heckscher–Ohlin (H–O) model that we discussed in Chapter 2. To reiterate, countries engage in trade when their factor endowments vary. If trading nations focus production on those activities that exploit their abundant factors intensively, gains from trade will follow. However, those gains will be distributed toward the owners of the abundant factors in each of the trading nations.

If we adapt the H–O model to the situation of trade between developing and developed countries, we might reasonably assume that developed nations are relatively abundant in high-skilled labor while developing countries are relatively abundant in low-skilled labor. Thus, the developed economies should focus on the production of high-skilled labor-intensive goods while their developing country trade partners should specialize in producing commodities that are low-skilled labor-intensive. Within developed economies, the consequence of such specialization is reduced demand for low-skilled, low-wage workers as the goods they produce are increasingly replaced by imports, while demand for the output of high-skilled workers should increase. The result is predicted to be rising wage inequality in developed countries and falling wage inequality in developing nations. What do the empirical data show?

An early series of papers (e.g. Borjas et al., 1992 and Lawrence and Slaughter, 1993) focused on accounting for the steep rise in US wage inequality through the 1980s. The three key explanatory factors were considered to be the immigration of low-skilled workers, rising trade and skill-biased technological change. The latter argument focuses on the introduction of new technologies into the economy, computers in the 1980s, and the idea that only workers with relatively high levels of human capital (education and skills) benefit from such technology. Most researchers at the time agreed that skill-biased technological change played the largest role in increasing wage inequality.

The general consensus today is that those early studies failed to capture the full impact of trade. The reason for this, at least in part, is that they imagined a simple H–O world where trade was dominated by the flow of finished goods produced in different industrial sectors characterized by their relative shares of low-skilled and high-skilled labor. The early models assumed that import competition would drive down relative commodity prices in industrial sectors dominated by low-skilled workers. The predicted change in commodity prices was not observed and thus trade was not considered a viable explanation for the growth of wage inequality. The central problem in these early studies was a search for the impacts of trade that focused on shifts in economic activity between rather than within industrial sectors. In the late-1990s, Feenstra and Hanson (1996) offered a model of international outsourcing in developed economies where industrial production was separated into two types of work, one performed by low-skilled labor and the other by high-skilled labor. As the global price of low-skilled labor declined relative to its domestic (developed country) price, so the share of low-skilled activity within all industries in developed economies was assumed to fall as low-skilled work was outsourced. The search for the impacts of trade thus shifted to a focus on intermediate goods, to changes in the shares of low-skilled and high-skilled work, and to wage divergence within rather than between industrial sectors.

The evidence in support of this model of international outsourcing is strong. Grossman and Rossi-Hansberg (2006) show that the import share of US manufacturing inputs more than doubled between 1972 and 2000, and Bernard et al. (2006) highlight the prominent rise of low-wage country imports to developed economies from the early 1990s. The rise in international outsourcing has been associated with the closure of domestic firms, significant job-loss and declining wages, especially for less-skilled workers (Kemeny et al., 2015; Klein et al., 2010; Rigby and Breau, 2008).

Within developing economies there is also mounting evidence that increased trade is correlated with rising inequality. Goldberg and Pavcnik (2007) provide an overview. The growth in inequality is sometimes linked to skill-upgrading within export-oriented firms (Verhoogen, 2008). In other cases, global competition and trade are blamed for eliminating small-scale producers in different economic sectors of the developing world, especially in agriculture. Competition between developing countries, South–South competition, also complicates the development paths of many poorer nations.

ETHICAL TRADE

Fair trade

As global production networks expand, the value chains that describe these networks also become more spatially fragmented. Recall that a value chain is made up of production, supply, marketing and distribution links that enable commodities to be manufactured and delivered to customers in markets around the world. Flows, transactions and trade between these links form economic and social relationships. A good example is the global value chain of coffee that ends in a cup of cappuccino at one of Starbucks's 21,300 worldwide stores. The economic and social life of the cappuccino begins with the farmer who grows coffee at one of the company's global sources from Costa Rica and Colombia in Latin America to Rwanda and Tanzania, Africa, and Yunnan, China. The coffee is imported and then sent to one of its five roasting plants in Nevada, Pennsylvania,

South Carolina, Washington and the Netherlands before it ends up at Starbucks' cafes and stores for consumption. Starbucks has pledged to treat its farmers ethically by sharing information on sustainable coffee growing, and promising a fair price. Starbucks' ethical trading behavior is described at its website (www.starbucks.com/coffee/ethical-sourcing).

Starbucks' pledge to conduct its coffee business more ethically is consistent with a growing trend among companies operating in many countries. As non-governmental organizations and labor activists press for a trading system that ensures a decent wage for farmer suppliers in developing countries, companies are also eager to show that they are socially responsible. The term "fair trade" was coined to describe this phenomenon. Initially promoted as alternative trade, the fair trade movement emerged over time as a way to alleviate poverty. According to Decarlo (2011: 2), "fair trade is a trading partnership, based on dialogue, transparency, and respect, that seeks greater equity in international trade". The goal of fair trade practitioners is to help farmers in poor countries to develop sustainable livelihoods by encouraging global companies to develop long-term cooperative relationships with the farmers. Rather than switch farmers quickly when they are dissatisfied with the product, companies work with farmers to develop quality products as Starbucks has pledged to do. Decarlo points out that not all companies that practice socially responsible business also practice fair trade. For example, a number of products have emerged on the market that are environmentally friendly and contribute to the greening of the economy. However, these companies would not be considered to engage in fair trade if their central mission does not target poverty alleviation. In this sense, fair trade integrates social and economic goals.

As the movement has gathered considerable momentum, the call for fairer trade has also become a call for greater trade justice in countries like Britain. What seems clear is that the movement is a reaction to perceived inequities generated by the free trade system, inequities that may be traced to the global core-periphery structure described in Chapter 5. Fair traders believe that factory workers in EPZs and poor farmers in Africa, Asia and Latin America should be treated more ethically by paying fair wages, ensuring safe working conditions and providing training that upgrades the skills of workers and farmers.

One outcome of the fair trade movement is that products have emerged that are fair trade certified. According to FairTrade USA, over 138 million pounds of coffee entering North America in 2012 were certified fair trade. Brands like Cafedirect, Coolearth Coffee and Eros Coffee have emerged in FairTrade UK that use the fair trade logo. It is not just coffee that is being sold with fair trade labels. Transfair USA, for instance, certifies nuts, cocoa, dried fruit, sugar, rice and other agro-food products. These products may now be found alongside conventional products on the shelves of Walmart, Whole Foods and Target, major retailers in the US. In Europe, companies like Cadbury chocolate and Nestlé have adopted fair trade certification for some of their products.

Biosecurity

In Chapter 4, we highlighted on-going trade conflict between the EU and the US over the safety of non-therapeutic hormone beef imports. Concern over the safety of the global food supply chain has now become a politically charged issue. In 2003, several countries imposed a ban on beef imports from North America following the detection of mad cow disease among US cattle. When the South Korean government lifted the import ban in 2008 it enraged thousands of Korean consumers who took to the streets to protest the decision. More recently, berries imported from China have been linked to cases of hepatitis A in Australia, prompting the company that imported the berries, Patties Food, to recall the berries. Meanwhile, in early 2015, China imposed controls on salmon imported from Norway citing worries that they carry a fish virus that potentially harms human health. In most of the cases, food safety concerns came on the heel of trade pacts. The US and South Korea, for example, had just concluded negotiations on the KORUS (Korea–US) free trade agreement in 2007, and opposition to US beef imports was influenced by Korean farmers' opposition to the agreement. Similarly, Australia signed a trade agreement with China that would boost agricultural exports and allow certain Chinese service contractors into the country. This raised concerns that the agreement would displace Australian workers. Not surprising, trade pacts have become politically charged as they increase competition for some sectors of the economy. More recently, opposition to various agricultural imports has also led to two complementary trends. The first is an assertion of the local scale as the preferred geographic scale for reconfiguring global food supply networks. The second, biosecurity, reinforces government and citizens' concern that a country's environment and its people's health should be protected from diseases, pollution and food contamination that spread through international trade.

To understand both, we need to return to the fair trade movement which represents a moral response to spatial and structural inequality that has developed as a result of core–periphery trade. Ethicists argue that rich and developed countries have a moral duty to repair harm arising from trade inequality by engaging in imports that will contribute to poverty alleviation in developing countries (Navin, 2014). However, the issue is much more complex. Take the case of biosecurity. The outbreak of epidemics has alerted citizens and governments to potential risks associated with cross-border movement of tainted agricultural and food products. Food security in particular is under surveillance for potential contamination by biological organisms (e.g. fungus or bacteria). A good example is the long-standing position adopted by the Australian government against the imports of New Zealand apples because of fear of fire blight from New Zealand. Fire blight is a bacterial disease that infects apples and pears. WTO members such as Australia are permitted to develop their own measures to assess food safety risks under the Sanitary and Phytosanitary Agreement. While a small amount of New Zealand apples is now permitted, they are subjected to a stringent protocol implemented by Australia to ensure that the apples are free of fire blight (Higgins and Dibden, 2011). The European Union has also instituted strict standards and regulations on food and agricultural imports. Labeling of food products must include information on genetically modified organisms (GMOs), allergens (e.g. gluten, peanuts), certain food colorings, aspartame and additives. Even global companies have joined the rush to biosecurity. McDonald's has decided to serve McNuggets and chicken burgers that are free of human antibiotics.

Concerns regarding food security have also spawned another movement, namely locavorism, which refers to the "buy local" food movement that is growing in North America and Europe. Since Michael Pollan (2006) published his popular book *The Omnivore's Dilemma*, urban farming and local farming have become coterminous with improved food security. While locavorism can protect consumers and the agricultural sector from foreign pests, organisms and environmental contamination, it is nevertheless a double-edged sword. Because agriculture is still an important sector among developing countries, buying local may act as a non-tariff barrier by discouraging American and European consumers from purchasing "distant food". Developing countries are not always able to meet food and agricultural standards imposed by North American or European countries. As an example, the EU banned shrimp imports from Benin in 2003 following the discovery of bacteria in a sample of Benin shrimp imports. The ban took a toll on the income of Benin's fishermen and fishmongers and the country as a whole, since the shrimp industry is a significant source of employment and foreign exchange revenue. The industry has not recovered even though the ban has been lifted (Houssa and Verpoorten, 2015).

Overall, ethical trade emerged to address injustices. In the case of fair trade, this injustice is addressed through better prices for poor farmers in developing countries. As for biosecurity and locavorism, the solution to what is often perceived as an unsustainable trade system lies in increased surveillance and the scaling down of food and agricultural production and trade. However, while the solutions are well-meaning, they can sometimes have unintended consequences. Higher coffee prices do not always make their way down the value chain to the farmer, as buyers possess the power to dictate and fix prices. Similarly, regulating the food trading system can be a guise for protectionism with negative consequences for poor countries.

ENVIRONMENT AND SUSTAINABILITY

The growth of the global economy places greater and greater demands on the environment. To the extent that trade can be linked to variations in economic growth and income levels around the world, it is implicated in debates around development, resource use and environmental quality. For some, these debates focus on **sustainable development**, how to organize social and economic life in ways that meet current needs while also protecting the ability of future generations to meet their needs, thus preserving the integrity of natural systems on which all life depends (Butlin, 1989). For others, the goals of development and environmental protection are antithetical and we are asked to pick one over the other. To complicate matters further, the physical and social systems that play central roles in these debates operate at different spatial scales (local, national and global) that make political regulation extraordinarily difficult. Given this complexity, it is little wonder that recent attempts to solve environmental concerns with trade policy have met with such animus.

For some environmentalists, then, growth and trade have only negative impacts on the environment and they call for putting a brake on the economy, limiting consumption and the production it demands. An alternative perspective suggests that trade can have a positive impact on the environment using markets to encourage competition and the more efficient use of resources, by diffusing "green" technologies around the world, and by raising incomes and generating the political will to manage the global environment. Cross-cutting these arguments are concerns over development and the environment that have an important spatio-political imprint. The richer, developed nations, where much of the impetus for environmental protection originates, express concern that developing nations exploit their comparative advantage in pollution (their lack of environmental regulations) to produce goods for the global economy without regard for the environmental consequences. It is these richer countries that increasingly insist on using trade policy as the vehicle to push a "green" agenda. However, just as in debates over the race to the bottom in terms of labor standards, developing countries cry foul. They view such policy as a form of **environmental colonialism** and they question the right of developed countries to legislate their prospects for development, especially as the industrialized nations of the world are responsible for most of the carbon dioxide trapped in the Earth's atmosphere.

In one sense assisting developing countries to raise incomes might have a positive impact on the environment. The desperate struggle of those living at the margins in the developing world contribute significantly to problems such as deforestation and desertification. Poorer and less well-educated people also tend to have higher fertility rates, with rising populations placing increasing pressure on fragile ecosystems. At higher levels of income, people tend to value the environment more positively, they demand cleaner air and water and they seem willing to pay for it in the form of taxes supporting government mandates to reduce pollution and protect natural resources. The relationship between environmental degradation and incomes is mapped in the **environmental Kuznets curve** (EKC) in Figure 6.3a. The EKC assumes that in the initial stages of industrialization, pollution and other forms of environmental degradation are likely to increase along with per capita incomes. With continued economic growth and resource shifts from more polluting to less polluting industrial sectors, rising incomes will have smaller and smaller negative impacts on environmental quality and will eventually reach a tipping point when further income gains will begin to lower environmental degradation.

There is reasonable evidence supporting the claims in the EKC, at least in terms of reducing industrial pollutants such as sulfur dioxide (Dinda, 2004), though whether the same relationship holds for natural resource use in general is less clear. The ability of richer countries to "export" pollution and other "environmental bads" by shifting heavy polluting industries and industrial waste to developing nations, perhaps to EPZs as discussed above, has given rise to the concept of the **ecological shadow**. Dauvergne (2008) uses this term to explain that rich, developed country populations are able to sustain high levels of consumption without destroying their local environment by relying on production (and environmental devastation) that takes place in other parts of the world. For example, the United States purchases large volumes of manufactured goods from China. The production of those goods generates an enormous amount of pollution. Some of that pollution is trapped in China, and some of it leaks out into the global environment. By importing Chinese goods, US consumers can reduce their exposure to environmental contaminants. The concept of ecological shadows is illustrated in Figure 6.3b in the map of carbon

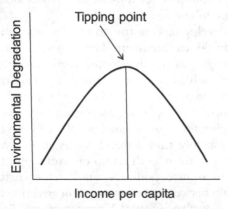

Figure 6.3 (continued)

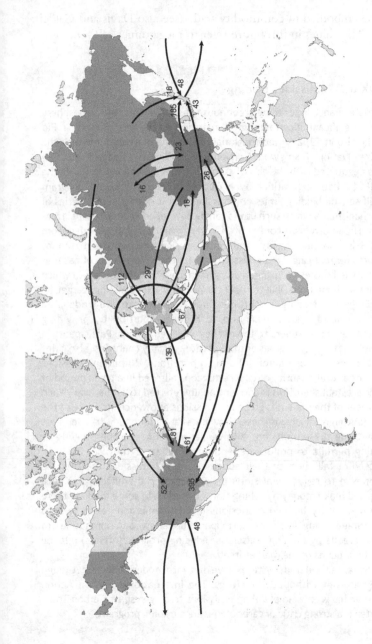

Figure 6.3 The environmental Kuznets curve and carbon dioxide trade flows

Source: The carbon dioxide flow map is adapted from Davis and Caldeira (2010).

dioxide embodied in commodity trade (see also Davis and Caldeira, 2010). The values in this figure refer to megatonnes of CO_2.

BOX 6.2   Emissions trading

Climate change induced by greenhouse gases (GHG) in the atmosphere poses significant uncertainty for humankind. At the Earth Summit in Rio de Janeiro in 1992 an international environment treaty known as the United Nations Framework Convention on Climate Change (UNFCCC) was negotiated with the aim of stabilizing GHG emissions. By 2015, the UNFCCC had been ratified by 197 countries. The framework program itself sets no binding limits on emissions but it does outline a series of mechanisms by which such limits can be developed in international treaties. The Kyoto Protocol adopted in Japan in 1997 and effective from 2005 is one such treaty that requires signing countries to adopt targets for reducing GHG emissions. So far the Kyoto Protocol has met with mixed success. Cap and trade systems are one of the ways in which countries hope to be able to meet their future GHG emissions targets.

Emissions trading, sometimes referred to as "cap and trade", is a market-based system designed to reduce pollution by providing incentives for members to lower their GHG emissions. Participants in emissions trading schemes or markets are typically countries (also cities and states such as California) and corporations. Within an emissions market a total quantity of GHG emissions allowed in a given period of time is established. This is conventionally referred to as the "cap". Each member of the market is given an emissions allowance, its share of the cap (in tougher systems these allowances are auctioned off). Members may trade these emissions allowances with one another, buying or selling permits to pollute depending on whether they are likely to exceed or fall short of their specific targets. Emissions markets are supposed to reduce emissions by encouraging members to pollute less and make money by selling unused credits. In some markets there are mandatory built in reductions in GHG emissions each year to encourage saving. In others, participants are allowed to purchase extra GHG credits by funding emissions reducing projects (offsets) outside the boundaries of the market itself.

So far cap and trade systems have met with moderate success, though they are not without their critics. The International Carbon Action Partnership is an example of an emissions trading system. Carbon Trade Watch is a strong critic of carbon emissions trading programs.

ENVIRONMENTAL POLICY AND TRADE AGREEMENTS

It remains unclear whether free trade is bad for the environment. However, environmental activists insist that the institutions that regulate international trade, first the General Agreement on Tariffs and Trade (GATT) and now the WTO, are committed to encouraging trade irrespective of its impact on the natural world. Chapter 4 provided a brief introduction to GATT and the WTO. These institutions are governed by a body of founding articles. Article XX of GATT outlines a series of instances in which WTO members may be exempt from the GATT rules that regulate international trade. The "green provisions" of Article XX state that WTO members may adopt domestic environmental legislation that is inconsistent with the general principles of GATT:

- If it is necessary to protect human, animal or plant life or health (paragraph b).
- Or relates to the conservation of exhaustible natural resources (paragraph g) . . . so long as these policies are not a "means of arbitrary or unjustifiable discrimination" or a "disguised restriction on international trade".

There has been much debate over the interpretation of Article XX, especially around two well-known cases involving the United States. At the core of the debate is whether a nation can impose restrictions on imported goods if the production of those goods violates domestic environmental law in the country of import. The two important cases are the tuna–dolphin case and the shrimp-turtle case.

In 1972 the United States government passed the Marine Mammals Protection Act (MMPA) in order to protect dolphins in the eastern tropical Pacific Ocean that were being killed in the nets of tuna fishing vessels. Though the ban requires US tuna fishing boats around the world to adopt dolphin-safe fishing practices, and it requires non-US vessels to do the same within US waters (up to 200 miles off the US coast), outside US waters fishing practices on foreign vessels are unrestricted. One of the consequences of the MMPA was for US fishing boats to "reflag" as ships registered outside the United States. Alarmed at the high number of dolphin deaths, in 1991 the US banned imports of tuna from Mexico and a number of other countries. Mexico protested to GATT and a dispute resolution panel ruled that the MMPA did not meet the dictates of Article XX and thus the US tuna import ban violated GATT. The environmental lobby protested to no avail. GATT decided that international trade restrictions could not be used by one country to impose its domestic environmental policy upon the production methods of other countries. In the end, strong consumer protests in the United States eventually won the day with tuna fisheries in both Mexico and the United States adopting dolphin-safe fishing practices.

A similar case in the 1990s brought a subtle difference in ruling from the WTO. Concerned that turtles were being caught in the nets of shrimp fishermen, the US used the Endangered Species Act of 1987 to demand that turtle excluder devices (TEDs) be fitted to shrimp fishing nets. Under Article XX of GATT, the US banned imported shrimp from India, Malaysia, Pakistan and Thailand because they did not use TEDs. These Asian countries protested to the WTO. Initially the United States lost the fight, with the WTO again arguing that environmental protections could not be used to undermine the basic principles of the international trading system. However, after a US appeal the language of the WTO shifted, claiming that sustainable economic development was consistent with the laws of international trade. In the end, the US still lost the case with the WTO ruling that insufficient time had been given to the Asian countries to adopt TEDs and that the import ban was therefore discriminatory. Once again, the US government was able to reach agreement with shrimp exporters to protect turtles, but the ruling of the WTO still inflamed tensions with environmentalists even though there had been a softening in the WTO's position.

BOX 6.3 Trade and the Arctic

With the relatively rapid retreat of sea-ice in recent years, the Arctic is the subject of much discussion as an alternative maritime trade route linking northern Europe and Northeast Asia, and as a site of significant natural resources. Recent research by Farre et al. (2014) indicates that before the construction of the Suez Canal, the standard journey between Rotterdam and Shanghai was about 14,000 nautical miles. Through the canal that journey is reduced to a little over 11,000 miles, but the Northern Passage through the Arctic could shorten the trip even further to about 8,000 miles. The appeal of a northern trade route, in terms of fuel-savings alone, is clear. If you think back to the gravity model of trade developed at the end of Chapter 2, a significant reduction in the distance between two trading nations will likely spur large increases in the volume of trade.

To some, then, the loss of Arctic sea-ice is a blessing. To others it is a curse, a bellwether of climate change already well underway and a looming environmental disaster in a pristine environment. The scramble by northern nations (Canada, Denmark (through Greenland), Norway, Russia and the United States) to assert control over territory across the Arctic signals their intent to pursue the oil and gas and mineral wealth of this region.

SUMMARY

In Chapter 2, we examined a series of models that showed the economic benefits or gains that emerge from trade. One of the models developed in that chapter, the H–O model, makes clear that the gains from trade are unlikely to be shared by all economic agents, and furthermore, that some groups might be negatively impacted by trade. In this chapter we explored some of the costs and benefits of trade in relation to labor and the environment.

Increased integration, supported by trade, has significantly changed economic activity around much of the world. From a series of relatively self-sufficient national economies that engaged in arms-length interactions, a great deal of production today is undertaken as parts of the supply chains of the TNCs that dominate the global economy. That integration has brought growth, alleviation of poverty (Chapter 5) and improved living conditions to many. For others, however, it has meant firm closure, job loss, deteriorating working conditions and declining wages. Reaching for a common denominator is not easy. For many, the linkages generated by increased trade mean greater opportunity along with greater competition and less certain futures.

One of the key sources of future uncertainty is climate change. The precise linkages between climate change and trade are not easy to draw. However, to the extent that economic growth rests upon global integration, then trade is clearly implicated in the rapid rise of greenhouse gas emissions and other forms of environmental degradation. Thus, while trade allows consumers to benefit from greater product variety and lower commodity prices in the short-run, the longer-run environmental costs of growth, rising incomes and greater and greater levels of consumption are likely to be high. With income inequality rising around much of the world, the ability of different groups and different countries to absorb those costs is going to be highly uneven.

The main points of this chapter are:

- Manufactures that do not require much skill or technology as inputs, in sectors such as clothing and footwear, are often concentrated in specialized areas called SEZs or EPZs in developing countries.

- Host countries offer generous incentives to TNCs to manufacture and export their products through EPZs. Much of the work in these zones is undertaken by women. EPZs can turn out to be isolated spatial enclaves with few linkages to the rest of the economy.

- The emergence of the global economy and the trade on which economic integration rests have profoundly altered labor markets around the world. More and more jobs are connected to the supply chains of TNCs. This means that workers around the world find themselves in greater competition with one another. This competition is associated with rising levels of wage inequality in developed and developing countries alike, and it has heightened concerns about the links between trade and the quality of work.

- Companies have responded to criticisms of unethical behavior by engaging in fair trade with the goal of helping poor farmers in developing countries achieve better prices and market access.

- Globalization through trade has generated new forms of conflict concerning food safety. Worries of food contamination by biological organisms have spawned local food movements in North America and Europe that discourage distant trade.

- The growth of trade and the emerging global economy have put increased pressure on the environment. More production means more consumption and greater use of resources. Can technological advancements and smart policy slow climate change?

- Disputes over the quality of work and the quality of the environment are increasingly being fought through trade institutions and in trade agreements.

SUGGESTED READING

Environment and Planning A and *Geoforum* journals
Students who wish to research more deeply the various topics of this chapter are encouraged to consult with articles published in these two journals. Topics on ethical trade and biosecurity are popular in the journals.

Najam, A., Halle, M. and Melendez-Ortiz, R. (eds.) (2007) *Trade and Environment: A Resource Book.* International Institute for Sustainable Development, International Center for Trade and Sustainable Development.
This book explores a series of discussions around trade and environment questions in a non-technical way. It provides a lot of case-study information drawn for different countries as well as an interesting focus on policy questions.

Werner, M. (2016) *Global Displacements: The Making of Uneven Development in the Caribbean.* Malden, MA and Oxford, UK: Wiley-Blackwell.
This book offers a critical look at the process of restructuring of garment production in the EPZs of the Dominican Republic and Haiti, driven by new WTO rules.

RESOURCES

The World Bank published "Development and Climate Change" in its 2010 report, addressing sustainability issues that include protection of the environment. OECD has many sections on its website addressing trade and climate change, trade and the environment, and trade and biosecurity (www.oecd.org/env/resources/). Both organizations collect environmental data which may be found at: http://data.worldbank.org/topic/environment and www.oecd.org/environment

The United Nations Conference on Trade and Development is also focused on the impacts of climate change in the developing world. In 2013, it published a trade and environment review entitled, *Wake Up Before it is Too Late: Make Agriculture Truly Sustainable Now For Food Security in a Changing Climate* (available at: unctad.org/en/PublicationsLibrary/ditcted2012d3_en.pdf).

Oxfam International, which is an organization that seeks to alleviate poverty in developing countries, frequently posts reports and statistics on trade and development.

The International Labor Organization is a useful source for information on labor rights and disputes around the world: http://www.ilo.org

The United Nations Framework Convention on Climate Change provides further information on the Kyoto Protocol and emissions trading on its website, http://unfccc.int/kyoto_protocol/mechanisms/emissions_trading/items/2731.php

CONCLUSION

International trade is an exciting field that is studied in many disciplines. Its impact is articulated at many geographical scales from the global to the local, in debates as broad as climate change, through international politics, to discussions about national and regional identity and to local concerns about how to make a living. Most often, these debates and the geographical scales at which they are focused are interconnected. The Greek crisis of 2015 and the departure of Britain from the EU illustrate such complexities. Greece's default on its payment to the International Monetary Fund (IMF) in 2015 triggered a continental crisis whose effect was felt in North America and East Asia. The crisis raised questions of national sovereignty and identity, and the difficulties of adjusting to austerity measures imposed from the outside, particularly from global agencies like the IMF and the European Central Bank, and from another country, in this case Germany. Meanwhile, the temporary closure of Greek banks had adverse effects on imports to and exports from the country. The crisis bit even deeper when shops, restaurants and hotels saw a sharp fall in service trade as cross-border travel to and from Greece slowed almost to a halt. A year later, Greece faced unprecedented flows of a very different sort. These flows of human refugees, in part prompted by an integrated European Union and the relative ease of crossing borders, are now generating calls for stronger border controls likely to restrict all forms of international movement in the future.

The 2015 events in Greece happened only one week after President Obama was given the authority to "fast-track" talks on the Trans-Pacific Partnership (TTP) with Asia, talks that have inflamed tensions among environmentalists, pro-labor groups and the general public (witness the presidential primary debates in 2016). The TPP initiative, from which China was purposely excluded, has prompted China to look west, back to the old Silk Road and connections between Asia and Europe as a way of shifting its focus from the United States and perhaps developing stronger partners closer to home. This is certainly one of the goals of the new Asian Infrastructure Investment Bank, increasingly seen as a Chinese alternative to the IMF and the World Bank. These events in Europe and on either side of the Pacific Ocean illustrate the importance of trade and the central role that it plays in directing the actions of nations, firms and individual people. Very few issues ignite the passion of policy-makers, government officials and ordinary citizens to the same extent as trade.

Throughout this book we have tried to emphasize that trade is not static. The nature of trade has shifted over time as the structure of the world economy has been pushed and pulled into new forms by processes of competition. Over the last few decades, transnational corporations (TNCs) have played a lead role in these processes, dramatically altering connections between different parts of the emerging global economy and the types of commodities that are being traded. New concentrations of capital and labor, new markets and new sites of profitable accumulation have emerged, just as established centers of economic activity and growth have declined. Alongside these changes come new tensions between those advantaged by the new poles of growth and those left behind. Whereas at one time these tensions might have mapped neatly into countries and industrial sectors, today they are much more complex reflecting the more fractured landscapes of winners and losers. In this final chapter of the book we seek to illustrate the dynamism of capitalist production and the trade on which it is based through exploring a series of debates that focus on new forms of trade.

TRENDS AND DIRECTIONS

Trade in energy: The case of solar energy

The beginning of 2015 saw a dramatic fall in the price of crude oil to less than US$50 per barrel. Until then, oil prices had exceeded

$100 per barrel for a number of years, peaking at nearly $150 in 2008. Energy is an essential input to industrialization. As more and more developing countries join the industrial revolution, demand for energy has increased. Since John Rockefeller assembled an empire selling oil in the nineteenth century, the petroleum industry has grown by leaps and bounds making up one-fifth of all international trade (including agriculture, manufacturing and services) today. However, as Chapter 6 demonstrated, concerns regarding climate change from greenhouse gas emissions have led to the search for alternative energy sources. There is some urgency in using energy that is renewable compared to fossil fuel that takes millions of years to form and that exacerbates air pollution. The four principle sources of renewable energy are hydro, wind, solar and biomass. This section will focus on solar energy because the industry captures some of the major themes detailed in this book.

As the world's largest producers of crude oil, the original twelve OPEC countries of Algeria, Angola, Ecuador, Iran, Iraq, Kuwait, Libya, Nigeria, Qatar, Saudi Arabia, United Arab Emirates and Venezuela have been major exporters of oil to the rest of the world for several decades. While this may change with the discovery of shale oil in the USA, contributing to over-supply that has resulted in falling oil prices, the role of OPEC is unlikely to diminish in the international trade of crude oil anytime soon. Competition for oil from resource-poor industrializing East Asia caused oil prices to boom in the 2000s. However, the same competitive pressures have forced many countries to turn to alternative sources to fuel their growth, including solar energy. There are also other incentives for turning to renewable solar energy: whereas coal was burnt to power steam engines during the eighteenth and nineteenth centuries, invention of the internal combustion engine rendered oil the more popular energy resource in the period following. Today, however, technologies associated with fossil fuel are becoming obsolete while new technologies are emerging in the renewable energy sector such as solar PV (photovoltaic). The trend towards renewable energy is also supported by greater awareness that a strategy of sustainable development will need to accompany the third industrial revolution that is associated with new sectors of economic growth such as communications and biotechnology. As countries push for a lower carbon footprint, solar energy has emerged a front-runner in the industrial policies of East Asia.

Table 7.1 shows that solar energy trade is dominated by China, Japan, South Korea, Malaysia and Germany today. These are all countries that are relatively poorly endowed in fossil energy. While China does have coal, its quality is not high. Coal has contributed to high levels of particulates (e.g. soot) and carbon dioxide, a greenhouse gas, in many Chinese cities. Consequently the Chinese government identified solar energy as one of its strategic industries. Likewise, Germany, Japan and South Korea are signatories of the Kyoto Protocol that seeks to reduce greenhouse gases. As major manufacturing powers with a prodigious need for energy, they too have turned to solar energy to fuel their domestic household and industrial needs. In Japan's case, the 2011 Fukushima nuclear incident incentivized the country's turn to solar energy. Consistent with strategic trade theory and industrial policy, developing the solar industry requires subsidies from the government. Among East Asian countries, the industry is also expected to spearhead technological progress that locates the countries as world-class innovators. The case of China is particularly interesting. China was not one of the top ten exporters of solar energy in 1990. By 2013, however, the trade value of its solar energy products had become larger than the next top four exporters combined. China also imports solar energy products capturing intra-industry trade within global value chains. Nonetheless, along with South Korea, it is one of few countries that enjoy a trade surplus in solar energy products. In this sense, export-promotion industrialization is increasingly associated with high-tech products that help to create dynamic comparative advantage.

China's current dominance in solar energy is supported by both domestic and foreign direct investments (FDI). The country receives nearly 35% of global renewable investment (Jordan, 2013). Domestically, it has favored policies that foster a cluster of firms specializing in PV cells while closing down power plants with outdated technology. Industrial policy is expressed through the 2006 Renewable Energy Law (amended in 2009) that obligates national power generating firms to purchase or generate a certain share of their power from renewable sources. At the same time, the government provides financial support to the industry including the initiation of two subsidy programs, the BIPV (building-integrated photovoltaics) and Golden Sun subsidy programs. Both were given up-front subsidies. For example, the government agreed to subsidize between 50% and 70%

Table 7.1 Solar energy trade among top ten countries, 1990 and 2013 (US$mi)

Importers				Exporters			
1990		2013		1990		2013	
Country	Value	Country	Value	Country	Value	Country	Value
Germany	188	China	8,994	Japan	360	China	15,795
Japan	85	Japan	7,007	Germany	151	Japan	4,726
South Korea	44	USA	5,791	Malaysia	61	South Korea	3,791
Singapore	39	Hong Kong	3,891	South Korea	57	Germany	3,490
Canada	30	Germany	3,546	Denmark	27	Malaysia	3,288
Switzerland	25	South Korea	3,302	Canada	22	Hong Kong	2,949
Malaysia	16	Mexico	1,463	Singapore	19	USA	2,243
Spain	14	UK	1,273	Thailand	15	Singapore	1,502
Brazil	14	Netherlands	1,149	Switzerland	5	Philippines	1,030
Mexico	11	India	1,069	Australia	3	Netherlands	966

Source: UN Comtrade

of solar power projects and power transmission systems. Industrial policy may be seen in financial assistance for PV applications such as designated solar PV buildings, and tax exemptions for PV products. As we pointed out earlier in Chapter 5, heavy government-supported exports have run into some trouble with the US and European Union slapping anti-dumping and anti-bribery charges on Chinese PV imports. Both had accused China of dumping solar PVs at below cost, thereby hurting their own manufacturers. Recognizing China's large market, EU governments opted for a more amicable settlement by agreeing to price floors. Under this deal, China will be able to meet half of the demand for solar PVs in Europe. The US, on the other hand, adopted a more hardline approach. It slapped up to 78% of anti-dumping duties onto solar panels made in China, reasoning that this will preempt tactics such as using parts made in Taiwan to avoid import tariffs. Government support also extends to other sources of renewable energy. Wind energy, for instance, enjoys local content requirements (LCR) that require a certain share of intermediate goods to be purchased from Chinese suppliers. LCR is a policy instrument of regional development since it attempts to create backward linkages between foreign and local firms.

Nonetheless, China is pressing ahead with the industry. And it is not the only country to do so. Germany, the US and Japan, all major exporters and importers of solar energy products, also support the industry through various means. These include: (i) the SunShot Initiative Scheme which provides grants for high-technology companies and consumer tax credits in the US; (ii) low-interest loans to consumers that install PV systems and tax credits (Germany); and (iii) installation cost subsidies for consumers (Japan) (Qiang et al., 2014). Together, these policies demonstrate the arguments implied in managed trade that greening the economy requires some level of assistance from the government as the process involves much research and development (R&D). Trade in renewable energy is expected to grow as more and more countries turn a green industrial policy towards a more sustainable global economy.

Trade in services

Trade in services has grown in the last two decades. The World Trade Organization (WTO) estimates that it now accounts for

20% of global trade and the service sector is responsible for one-third of employment around the world. Services cover a range of industries from transportation, construction, health, education, professional services (legal and accounting) to communication, finance, insurance, royalties and computer information services. Spurred by declining communication costs, banks, logistical, consulting and professional firms are offering services across borders that help to promote the international trade of services.

The growing importance of services trade may be seen in the fact that the sector now accounts for 72% and 53% of high-income and middle-income countries' gross domestic product (GDP) (Cattaneo et al., 2010). The importance of this sector to countries like the United States should not be under-estimated given the size of the US trade deficit in the goods sector. Indeed a rather unusual situation has arisen here: the US has a trade surplus in the service sector, but this is the opposite for Japan, China and Germany, which have a trade deficit in services but a trade surplus in the manufacturing sector. The US is joined by France and the UK, among the G-7 countries, in terms of running a surplus in services trade. A significant share of services in these three economies is transacted through their TNC affiliates in host countries. Large service providers in the financial, accounting or legal sector often favor face-to-face contact with their clients. This means that they will set up affiliate offices in foreign countries to service the American, French, German, Japanese or English companies that are there, or to service other foreign companies. The largest services trade flows occur between North America and Europe, which export and import roughly a third of total global service trade from one another.

One major driver of the services trade is international finance, which has become an important component of the global economy. While international trade and investment have facilitated growth of the contemporary global economy, financial transactions have exploded and their effect is keenly felt by countries from Asia to North America to Europe, both in periods of expansion and, perhaps more especially, during episodic downturns. Large transnational banks like HSBC, Citigroup, JP Morgan, Bank of Tokyo-Mitsubishi UFJ and Deutsche Bank have established offices worldwide to serve corporations. Cross-border trade often involves capital movement as part of the provision of services; hence finance including credit, insurance and securities trading has become highly tradeable. Insurance and banking can be traded in the following ways: when a foreign supplier sells services to consumers of a domestic territory, or when a foreign firm establishes a subsidiary in the host country through FDI and sells services to domestic consumers. Unlike manufacturing, which has seen a more multi-regional distribution of production along continental lines, export of financial services remains heavily controlled by firms from countries of North America and Europe. Approximately thirty countries from these two regions are responsible for 80% of world trade in services (WTO, 2013). However, financial trade is also regulated. Regulations may arise from licensing requirements, or controls on ownership and allowable activities. Consequently, the industry, particularly firms originating from the West, has been active in pressing for financial liberalization. The General Agreement on Trade in Services (GATS) came into force in 1995 and contains a set of rules that target further liberalization of finance. Most of the rules focus on granting greater access to markets and the entry of foreign firms. However, governments recognize that unlike the goods sector, national regulation of the service industry may be necessary in some industries. For example, accountants and doctors are licensed differently in different countries. Nonetheless, the WTO is cognizant of barriers such as restrictions of labor mobility or domestic monopolies of the communication and transportation industries. It has tried, under GATS, to promote better management of migration that does not discriminate against foreign firms. However, such obligations are difficult to enforce since the organization recognizes that its members are faced with citizenship and domestic employment problems.

Trade in ideas

Long-run economic growth and increases in average income (GDP per capita) are crucially dependent upon technological change. This is true for both rich and poor economies. While less-developed countries can enjoy substantial growth through shifting resources from less to more productive sectors, sustained gains rely on technological upgrading. For advanced, industrialized economies, knowledge production is really the only game in town. While there are many competing frameworks for thinking about the economy and development, almost all agree on the central role of technology to the process of growth. Here we understand knowledge production as the creation of new ideas and technology as the application of those ideas within the economy.

Knowledge is a very special commodity. Unlike most other goods, knowledge is generally recognized as being **non-rival**, meaning that one firm's consumption of knowledge does not prevent others from using that same knowledge. Water is a classic example of a rival good. When a consumer drinks a bottle of water, that bottle of water cannot be consumed by someone else. Knowledge is also partly **non-excludable**. Excludable goods are those for which consumption is limited to those who purchased them. Goods that are non-excludable may be consumed by individuals who did not buy them. Commodities that are non-rival and non-excludable are typically referred to as **public goods**. If knowledge was a pure public good, no firms would have an incentive to develop it. Different kinds of knowledge, or intellectual property, are protected by institutions such as patents, copyrights and trademarks. Patents reward and encourage invention of new products and processes of production by restricting the gains from exploiting those technologies to those who invented them, at least for a certain period of time. Copyrights protect different kinds of knowledge, typically that knowledge which generates an artistic product such as a film, a book or a piece of music. Trademarks are identifying names or logos that are registered by producers or merchants. Trademarks are often associated with product quality from which owners are able to generate rents. Trademarks are carefully guarded against imitation. Owners of patents, copyrights and trademarks can sell, or license, the use of the products they have created under specified conditions. It is important to note that most kinds of knowledge are not fully excludable even when subject to **intellectual property rights** protections. Books and music are illegally copied and consumed by many, just as brand-name products are imitated by cheap "knock-offs". Similarly, new technologies are regularly copied by firms as part of the process of competition.

The nature of knowledge and technology means that they can be obtained in many different ways. They can be produced directly in a process that we conventionally label R&D. Alternatively, they can be purchased in the market. Some firms license the rights to deploy particular technologies. For example, pharmaceutical firms sell their formulae for specific drugs to other firms that seek to produce generics. Yet other firms acquire technology that is embodied in goods traded in the market. Thus, when Dell sells one of its computers that contains a central processing unit (CPU) manufactured by Intel, it relies on the technology that Intel embedded in that CPU. Trade in machinery and tools is a critical means for emerging economies to access the technologies they might not yet be able to produce themselves. That machinery might be employed directly in the production of still other goods, or it might be disassembled in a process of reverse engineering to expose the technology upon which it is based. Knowledge production is very expensive and very risky, hence reverse engineering is a smart alternative to R&D, especially for developing economies that do not possess the technological know-how to develop sophisticated products (Bell and Pavitt, 1997). Japan and Korea relied heavily on reverse engineering to catch up to global technology leaders in a relatively short span of time. Now they are at the technological frontier and must pay greater attention to guarding the technology that they produce, as countries like China and India follow hard on their heels. Technology is also embodied in the flows of labor that take place between firms and countries. As workers, particularly skilled employees, move from job to job they take skills and knowledge of technologies learned in one firm and location to another firm in a similar or distant location. The international movement (trade) of students from country to country, as part of their education, is a prominent example of labor mobility and knowledge acquisition, connected to debates over "brain drain" and "brain gain". The governments of many developing economies send their students to universities in developed countries in order to access new technology. Many such students remain in industrialized nations often leveraging their skills in new technology ventures before returning to their home countries to exploit their skills in new environments (see Saxenian, 2007).

The international literature on trade and technology development focuses on two main mechanisms of knowledge accumulation. In the first, trade is assumed to change patterns of specialization, pushing countries to develop economic sectors that have greater potential for technological growth. Technological upgrading and productivity growth are largely seen as domestic in this framework, occurring through different learning processes. In the second, trade in intermediate goods is seen as the source of technological inputs that fuel the growth process. In related empirical work Coe and Helpman (1995) show that the productivity growth of OECD (Organisation for Economic Co-operation and Development) countries depends on knowledge stocks developed domestically and on the stocks of knowledge developed by a country's most important trading partners. More recent work suggests that technology flows embodied in North–South trade have a positive influence on economic growth in developing economies (Falvey et al., 2002). The types of knowledge that can be moved over space and the influence of geographical distance on those flows are examined by Maskell and Malmberg (1999) and Jaffe and Trajtenberg (1999). Cohen and Levinthal (1990) argue that the ability of countries to use foreign technology depends on their **absorptive capacity**, on their ability to identify the technology embodied in goods traded and on whether they have the institutional capacity to leverage that technology and employ it productively. Newer work by Hidalgo et al. (2007) suggests that absorptive capacity also depends upon the "distance" between technologies that are found in different types of commodities. Thus, countries are seen as building competence in the production of certain kinds of commodities and their potential to diversify and upgrade is limited by the "technological relatedness" of different kinds of products. Technology gaps between developed and developing countries are explored in UNCTAD (2014b).

TNCs are a major channel for transferring technology between countries. UNCTAD (1997) estimates that over 80% of royalty payments for international technology transfers were made between TNC subsidiaries and their parent firms. The bigger question is whether technology transfers within TNCs spill over to domestic firms in host economies. Empirical work reveals that TNC affiliates are more productive than domestic firms in the same sector and that there is little evidence of spillovers (UNCTAD, 2014a). Furthermore, the higher productivity TNC affiliates drive up competition for domestic firms and force many from the market. This has generated significant concerns in the agricultural sectors of developing economies regarding food security. A closely related literature explores whether firms learn through trade, for instance by operating in export markets. The bulk of the evidence suggests that they do not.

Firms that engage in trade are more productive than firms in general, but these productivity differences typically precede international activity.

BOX 7.1 Trade-related aspects of intellectual property rights (TRIPS)

Broad recognition of the importance of knowledge to economic growth has generated demands for international regulation to protect intellectual property (IP) rights in trade agreements. Just as in the cases of labor and environmental regulation explored in Chapter 6, protecting knowledge has generated tensions between developed and developing countries. For the advanced, industrialized countries, where much of the world's knowledge production remains concentrated, IP protection is seen as central to maintaining competitive advantage. In developing economies, bolstering such protections is widely regarded as contributing to the **development deficit**, limiting access to education and technology especially in sensitive areas such as healthcare, agriculture and food production. Adding fuel to the fire, Birdsall et al. (2005) note that many industrialized economies used relatively weak IP protections in early stages of their own development to encourage the growth and diffusion of technological capabilities. Only as they shifted from being consumers of technology to producers have these countries demanded greater IP protection. At the core of international debates around IP rights is the question of whether emerging economies today should have the same flexibility. Richards (2005) provides an engaging overview of the different arguments in this debate.

In 1994, at the end of the Uruguay Round of General Agreement on Tariffs and Trade (GATT) negotiations, an international accord on Trade-Related Aspects of Intellectual Property Rights (TRIPS) was reached. Now administered by the World Trade Organization (WTO), TRIPS introduced IP protections into the global trading system with the aim of promoting the development of innovation and the dissemination of technology around the world. Developed countries pushed hard for TRIPS to be tied to the WTO assuring that disputes would be handled by the standard settlement procedures of this body. A requirement of WTO membership is ratification of the TRIPS agreement. Concerns over the impact of TRIPS on developing countries, particularly in the field of public health, led to the Doha Declaration in 2001 that specified nation-states should not be prevented from dealing with public health crises. However, policy accommodations were still required to be consistent with TRIPS provisions. This is interpreted by many to suggest that TRIPS requirements are broad and binding.

The WTO and its developed country members had argued that TRIPS would speed the flow of new technology to poorer countries around the world, either through trade or through foreign direct investment. To date, the evidence supporting these claims is mixed (UNCTAD, 2010). Indeed, TRIPS has been blamed for slowing the development of generic drugs across some developing countries, though low cost AIDS related medicines were ultimately approved for distribution across sub-Saharan Africa. A number of transnational corporations have recently shifted parts of their research and development operations into a small number of developing countries, perhaps in response to changing institutional regimes that favor IP protections. The impacts of these changes on development prospects remain unclear at this time.

Much remains unknown about knowledge production and the geographical mobility of technology. What types of knowledge are most valuable, where is that knowledge produced and what are the conditions of its production? How mobile are different forms of knowledge, how effective is trade at diffusing technological knowledge and how do firms and countries source knowledge and technology around the world? These are some of the most actively discussed questions by economic geographers, trade economists and related researchers today.

Trade in the developing world (South–South trade)

World trade data from UNCTAD (see Figure 7.1) show that the value of exports between developing countries (South–South trade, here not strictly limited to developing countries of the southern hemisphere) surpassed the value of exports from developing countries to developed countries (South–North trade) around 2008. The growth of consumption, as well as production, across the economies of the developing world over the last few decades is remarkable. Indeed, since 2000 the growth of exports from developing to developed countries has eclipsed the growth of exports between

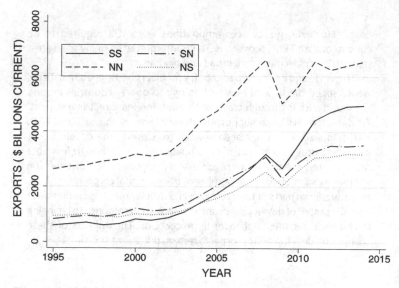

Figure 7.1 Global trade of North and South

Source: UNCTAD database (unctadstat.unctad.org)

developed economies. What remains unclear, however, is the extent to which these changes signify the growth of final goods markets in developing countries as opposed to the increasing role that developing countries play in the complex global value chains and production networks of TNCs that still tend to be dominated by lead firms from developed nations.

Questions regarding the precise role of developing countries within the global economy notwithstanding, there can surely be little question that the global South is going to assume a much more significant position in the future. This is made clear in the United Nations Human Development Report of 2013 that charts the rapid pace of economic growth and improvement in development indicators across much of the developing world over the last two to three decades (UNHDR, 2013). To be sure, the lives of billions of people across the developing countries of the world are still immensely difficult, but the broad improvement in development indicators for almost all countries included in UN surveys since the early 1990s is dramatic. The UNHDR notes that today, the combined

GDP of the three largest developing economies—Brazil, China and India—is about equal to that of Canada, France, Germany, Italy, the United Kingdom and the United States. In 1950, Brazil, China and India produced only about 10% of world GDP, while the developed nations just listed generated about half the world's output. In 2012, the developing world as a whole produced approximately 50% of world GDP, up from 35% or so in 1990. At least part of these rapid gains is associated with demographic shifts. Defining a global middle class as people earning or spending between $10 and $100 a day (in 2005 purchasing power parity terms), it is estimated that just over half of the world's middle class live in the developing nations of the world today. That share is expected to rise to 80% by 2030, with well over half of that group in China and India alone. This is a market that no TNC can ignore.

Horner (2015) suggests that these shifts in development raise a series of intriguing possibilities regarding the relations between different parts of the global economy that have been relatively stable for such a long time. For some, new geographies of trade and FDI herald the emergence of a distinctive "South–South" space of partnerships among equals. Carmody (2011) is somewhat more pessimistic, envisioning novel forms of neo-colonialism especially in the scramble for global resources. Recent Chinese and Indian investments in Africa are reminiscent of the power-asymmetries that shaped earlier forms of colonial development (McCann, 2010). Finally, significant attention is shifting to the global value chains and production networks that integrate economic activity across parts of the global South. Kaplinsky and Farooki (2011) ask how will these networks be organized in the future, where will the lead firms that control them be located and how will prospects for value-chain upgrading be distributed over space? Glassman (2011) questions how the geopolitics within and between competing nations of the global South might shape the governance of these networks.

At this time, we do not have enough information to hazard much of a guess about these questions. How the global economy will be transformed and what role different economies will play in the future are largely unknown. A fair bet, perhaps, is that recent history might not provide many clues to future trajectories of economic growth and national fortunes.

SUMMARY

In this book we have tried to give a flavor of the growing importance of trade around the world. We have explored the core of trade theory and its extensions to new models of global outsourcing. We have examined the changing structure of trade agreements and the incorporation of non-trade regulations within those agreements. The influence of transnational corporations on trade flows and the links between the activities of TNCs, trade, growth and development are core issues that occupy individual chapters in this book.

Each of the topics that we have addressed could quite easily be expanded into independent book length projects. Our aim has been to provide an accessible introduction to international trade and of the links between trade and other core components of the global economy.

The significance of trade within our world has, perhaps, never been higher. At the same time, our ability to unpack the impacts of trade in different parts of the global economy is severely compromised by trade data that obscure the activities of individual firms and countries. Who gains and who benefits from trade are enduring questions that continue to provoke academic and public debate. In this final chapter we have highlighted some of the key emerging themes that are frequently linked to trade. This is, of course, but a partial listing, though we hope that it is suggestive of the significance of flows within the global economy and of the importance of understanding the connections between people, places and processes that structure the world(s) that we make.

The main points of this chapter are:

- The nature of trade has shifted over time as the structure of the world economy has been pushed and pulled into new forms by processes of competition. Over the last few decades, TNCs have played a lead role in these processes, dramatically altering connections between different parts of the emerging global economy and the types of commodities that are being traded.
- Alongside these changes come new tensions between those advantaged by the new poles of growth and those left behind.

Whereas at one time these tensions might have mapped neatly into countries and industrial sectors, today they are much more complex reflecting the more fractured landscapes of winners and losers.

- We provide four examples of new forms of trade that illustrate the dynamism of the nature and the structure of international flows of goods and services. First, we illustrate the significance of solar energy as a green technology that has become central to the efforts of many economies to push towards a smaller environmental footprint. The role of policy in nurturing this infant industry is illustrated across leading solar energy manufacturers. Second, we highlight the growth of services trade and, specifically, the role of finance in fueling new trade flows and patterns of FDI around the global economy. Third, we explore the nature of technology and the rising importance of knowledge flows around the world. Fourth, we outline the growing importance of South–South trade or trade between developing economies. The weight of the global South within the world economy as a whole has increased sharply over the last few decades and there seems to be broad agreement that this pattern will continue. How this change will alter the pattern of world trade and trade relationships between different groups of countries remains unclear at this time.

SUGGESTED READING

Saxenian, A. (2007) *The New Argonauts: Regional Advantage in a Global Economy.* Cambridge, MA: Cambridge University Press

In this book, Saxenian links the advantages of a region in a country to transnational brain circulation. Using the example of entrepreneurs from countries like Taiwan, China and India, and their linkages to Silicon Valley, she makes the argument that skilled labor mobility can be a source of dynamic regional economic development.

UNCTAD (2010) *Intellectual Property in the World Trade Organization.* New York: United Nations.

UNCTAD (2014b) "Transfer of technology and knowledge sharing for development." *UNCTAD Current Studies on Science, Technology and Innovation* # 8. New York: United Nations.

UNHDR (2013) *United Nations Human Development Report: The Rise of the South.* New York: United Nations.

RESOURCES

Two impressive websites that explore the composition of exports from different
countries and the possibilities for technological upgrading in those countries
are the Atlas of Economic Complexity (http://atlas.cid.harvard.edu/) and the
Observatory of Economic Complexity (http://atlas.media.mit.edu/en/)

In addition, check out WTO TRIPS Gateway at: www.wto.org/english/
tratop_e/trips_e/trips_e.htm and United Nations Office for South–South
Cooperation at: www.google.com/?gws_rd=ssl#q=global+south

GLOSSARY

Absolute advantage: The country that can produce a commodity most efficiently is said to have an absolute advantage in the production of that commodity. Absolute advantage was the basis for free trade according to Adam Smith.

Absorptive capacity: The ability of firms and countries to identify technological opportunities and leverage those opportunities productively.

AFTA (ASEAN free trade area):   A free trade area in Southeast Asia comprising the countries of Brunei Darussalam, Cambodia, Indonesia, Laos, Malaysia, Myanmar, the Philippines, Singapore, Thailand and Vietnam.

APEC: Asia-Pacific Economic Cooperation. An organization consisting of twenty-one countries around the Asia-Pacific ocean whose mission is to enhance trade and economic prosperity in the region.

Bilateralism: The political, economic, trading and cultural relationship of two countries.

Biosecurity: Surveillance and preventive measures to control the spread of biological organisms (e.g. microbes, bacteria, virus) and diseases to plants, agriculture, livestock and also human health.

Cap and trade: A market-based system designed to reduce pollution by providing incentives for members to lower greenhouse gas (GHG) emissions. The cap limits total GHG emissions allowed over some period, and members may trade emissions credits with one another.

Comparative advantage: Comparative advantage exists when the opportunity costs of producing commodities vary between countries. Even if one country has an absolute advantage in producing all commodities compared with a second country, these nations can still benefit from trade if there are differences between the countries in the relative efficiency with which they can produce different commodities. Countries can benefit from free trade if they export commodities in which they have the largest relative efficiency advantage and import commodities in which they have the smallest relative efficiency advantage.

Constructivism: A theory of institutionalism that views the development of pan-regional institutions as arising from the social interactions of economic agents and the latter's learning effects.

Core–periphery: Describes the hierarchical structure of the world economy where the concentration of trade benefits, and thereby economic power, lies in industrial centers (core). Developing countries on the periphery, on the other hand, produce food and raw materials for industrial centers. Technical progress at the industrial centers helps their population to sustain itself. But the inability of developing countries to share in the benefits of technical progress at the core keeps them spatially embedded at the periphery.

Countervailing duties: Import duties imposed to counter the negative effect of subsidies by an exporting country.

Currency war: Popularized by Brazil's finance minister Guido Mantega in 2010, the term refers to competitive currency devaluation between countries in order to boost exports.

Customs union: Agreement between a group of countries to lower trade barriers among members as well as to adopt a common external tariff regarding imports from non-members.

Deindustrialization: The decline in the share of manufacturing employment within countries.

Developmental state: Theory developed by Chalmers Johnson (1982) to explain Japan's economic development. Johnson maintains that Japan's post-war economic emergence may be explained by technocratic competency and rules of the game that favor cooperation between government and business.

Dumping/anti-dumping: Dumping occurs when the price of an export is lower than the price at the home country. Anti-dumping refers to actions (tariff) that an importing country may undertake to offset the dumping of a good.

Dynamic comparative advantage: Transformation of a country's comparative advantage and competitiveness over time because of changes in wage, investment, resources, human capital, economies of scale and technological progress.

Ecological shadow: The movement of high polluting industries from high-income economies to low-income economies. The result is that high-income economies can maintain high levels of consumption while maintaining environmental quality at the expense of poorer nations.

Economic union: A high level of regional integration involving economic coordination between state members in matters of fiscal and monetary policies. The best example is the European Union where monetary union has resulted in a single currency.

Entrepot trade: Re-exports and transshipment of goods. For example, a significant amount of goods that are imported by entrepot centers like Hong Kong are stored and then re-exported again.

Environmental colonialism: The imposition of environmental restrictions on emerging economies by industrialized nations. These restrictions are often linked to trade agreements.

Environmental Kuznets curve: A hypothesized relationship between environmental degradation and per capita income within an individual country. At low levels of income, growth and development lead to deteriorating environmental quality. Once income reaches a certain point and the environment is more highly valued, further income gains are thought to be associated with improving environmental quality.

Export processing zone: See special economic zones.

Export promotion: When a country favors an industrial strategy that reduces its export bias (e.g. quantitative restrictions) in order to encourage its domestic firms to sell goods and commodities to the rest of the world.

European Commission: This is the executive and administrative arm of the EU. It consists of twenty-eight commissioners that are appointed by national governments, each with a specific service area.

European Council: The legislative arm of the European Union comprising of state representatives from member states. It is the last stop for EU policy-making as it makes the final decisions on policies and Treaty amendments.

European Parliament: A parliament that is made up of some 751 members who are elected from the twenty-eight EU countries. The institution helps to amend legislation, appoint members to other institutions and also control the EU budget.

Factor price equalization: This trade theorem states that even if factors of production (inputs to production) are immobile, free trade leads not only to convergence in the prices of commodities traded in international markets but also to a convergence in the prices of the factors that are used to produce commodities that are traded.

Foreign affiliates: Foreign firms in which a TNC has at least a 10% equity stake.

Foreign direct investment: Capital investment that flows from one country to another in order to control value adding activity in the destination.

Free trade: When countries trade without resorting to restrictions in the form of tariffs or non-tariff instruments.

Free trade area (FTA): Consists of a group of countries that have agreed to lower their tariffs and non-tariff barriers with one another. Such an agreement does not extend to non-members.

G-7: A group of powerful countries comprising seven members, namely Canada, Italy, Germany, France, Japan, the UK and the US. Finance ministers of the group meet regularly to discuss economic issues.

General Agreement on Tariffs and Trade (GATT): A contract between countries (often called contracting parties) to secure an environment that facilitates unrestricted trade and investment.

Global commodity chain: See global production network.

Global production network: Because the production activities of firms increasingly occur as "tasks", they may be broken up and be outsourced to different countries. In turn, spatial fragmentation spurs trade-in-value (see global value chain). Such a view favors looking at trade between firms or within firms as part of a larger network that supports the global trade economy.

Global value chain: The range of activities undertaken by firms to bring a product or service to the market. This can include design, production (e.g. providing resources or inputs, assembling component, etc.), marketing and distribution. The concept implies that the value of a product or service increases as it moves up the chain towards completion for end-use.

Gravity model: The gravity model is a simple framework that explains the extent of interaction between two objects (countries) as a positive function of the mass of those objects and an inverse function of the distance between them. It is sometimes used to predict the amount of trade between two countries.

Heckscher-Ohlin model: A two-country, two-commodity and two-input trade model often deployed to examine the influence of trade on relative factor prices. The core of the model suggests that countries should export the commodity that uses their abundant factor of production intensively. The influence of trade on factor prices in this model is explained through factor-price equalization and the Stolper-Samuelson theory.

Import-substitution: When a country substitutes its exports with imports. This may be used as an industrial strategy to develop domestic goods and manufactures.

Industrial policy: When a country engages in policies that accelerate the development of an industry deemed to be central to the country's establishment of a manufacturing base and technological catch-up. Such policies may involve government subsidies or other protection.

Leontieff's paradox: Wassily Leontieff was an economist who engaged in a simple test of the Heckscher-Ohlin (H-O) trade model using data for 1947. He calculated that the US was abundant in capital relative to the rest of the world and therefore that the US should export capital-intensive goods and import labor-intensive goods. He found the capital–labor ratio of imports to be greater than that for exports, seemingly contradicting the dictates of the H-O framework.

Local content requirement: A policy instrument to ensure that a certain percentage of intermediate goods in the production process is manufactured by domestic or local companies.

Locavorism: Describes the local food movement. Motivated by concerns of environmental and health, a locavore is an individual who is committed to eating food that is grown at a localized scale, usually within 100 miles.

Managed trade: Refers to the notion that international trade occurs in imperfectly competitive environments, hence producers of certain sectors, particularly high-tech sectors, can reap above- average profits. To do so, trade should be managed (e.g. through government assistance) so that countries do not lose their markets to competitors.

Mercantilism: Refers to merchant capitalism where trade and commerce are seen by its practitioners to be a source of value that could help strengthen the state. Historically, state power is achieved through accumulation of precious metals. In the contemporary context, East Asia's mercantilism is frequently associated with its vast foreign exchange reserves that support state power.

MERCOSUR: Also known as the Common Market of the South, the trade bloc consists of the countries of Argentina, Brazil, Paraguay (currently suspended) and Uruguay. The bloc has recently adopted rules to realize its customs union goal. Venezuela is in the process of joining the regional bloc.

Middle-income trap: Countries are said to be in the middle-income trap when they have shifted production from primary to industrial activity and they have expanded income per capita. These nations often struggle to remain competitive as wages are rising, lacking the diversification and advanced technologies of high-income economies.

Monopolistic competition: A form of imperfect competition that underpins intra-industry trade. In these models firms compete with one another by producing different varieties of the same product. Firms have some control over market prices and they enjoy increasing returns to scale. Consumers gain from the greater variety of products offered for sale in each industry. These models are typically developed to account for the growth of trade between countries with similar factor endowments and technologies.

Multilateral trade: Under a multilateral trade system, countries will trade with many other countries in the world. The World Trade Organization is responsible for coordinating multilateral trade agreements.

NAFTA: An acronym for the North America Free Trade Agreement. The Agreement created a free trade area consisting of three countries, namely the United States, Canada and Mexico.

Neofunctionalism: This theory maintains that if countries are trading significantly with one another, then consolidating trade relationships through supra-national institutions will lead to greater trade predictability by lowering transaction costs.

Neoliberalism: A branch of institutional analysis whose theoretical origin may be traced to the assumption that all economic actors are self-interested. Since institutions develop language to codify rationality as part of meaning-making, actors also build institutions to maximize those self-interests.

New trade theory: That branch of trade theory that rests upon monopolistic competition. According to this framework, firms offer slightly different commodity variants for sale in markets over which they exert some control over prices. Increasing returns to scale are frequently assumed to explain patterns of specialization. Trade occurs in this model even between countries that have relatively similar factor endowments and technologies.

New, new trade theory: A new model of trade that post-dates new trade theory that is built around the concept of heterogeneous firms, and that is often deployed to explain international offshoring.

Non-tariff barrier: When trade is restricted using instruments such as subsidies, voluntary export restraints and quotas.

Perfect competition: The standard model of competition characterized by the presence of large numbers of firms in each industry. These firms are assumed to have no control over market prices: they are price-takers.

Prebisch-Singer hypothesis: Suggests that the terms of trade for primary goods will deteriorate in relation to manufactured goods over time.

Regionalism: In geographic research, regionalism describes the relationships (local and extra-local) that influence the assembling of a region. Here geographers focus on regional assemblage at the sub-national level. In international trade scholarship, regionalism more commonly refers to the analysis of regional integration between member countries.

Regionalization: When countries increase their trade intensities with one another without formalizing the relationships. Regionalization of trade typically occurs between countries that are located close to one another.

Special economic zones (SEZs): Protected areas that act as free trade zones within a country. Imports in these areas typically face zero or marginal tariffs. Tariff reduction and other incentives (e.g. low corporate taxes) are offered to attract foreign multinational companies. Most of the goods produced in these zones are destined for world markets.

Stolper-Samuelson theorem: This theorem is typically associated with the Heckscher-Ohlin trade model. It states that as trade alters commodity prices it leads to an increase in the real earnings of the factor used intensively to produce the commodity whose price is increasing, and a decrease in the real earnings of the factor used to produce the commodity whose price is decreasing.

Strategic trade policy: Refers to trade policy that can benefit a country by influencing the shifting profits from foreign to domestic firms. An example of such a policy is subsidies to research and development or export subsidies for firms that face global competition.

Sustainability: The organization of social and economic life to meet current needs while protecting the integrity of natural systems.

Tariff: A form of restrictive trade through an import tax.

Terms of trade: The value of one bundle of goods in terms of another bundle of goods. It is commonly expressed for an individual country as the ratio of the prices of commodities exported to the prices of commodities imported.

Transnational corporation: A corporation that owns or controls value adding activity in more than one country.

Transnationality index: A measure of the extent to which a transnational corporation's activities are distributed outside the country where it is headquartered. The index is often calculated as an average of the ratio of foreign assets to total assets, the ratio of foreign sales to domestic sales, and the ratio of foreign employment to total employment.

WTO (World Trade Organization): An organization established in 1995 to govern world trade. Members (around 162 in 2015) that have ratified its rules agree to the organization's guidelines regarding the regulation of multilateral trade.

BIBLIOGRAPHY

Acemoglu, D., S. Johnson and J. Robinson. "The rise of Europe: Atlantic trade, institutional change and economic growth." *American Economic Review* 95 (2005): 546–79.

Acharya, A. "How ideas spread: Whose norms matter? Norm localization and institutional change in Asian regionalism." *International Organization* 58 (2004): 239–75.

Adewale, A.R. "Does import-substitution industrialization strategy hurt growth?" *African and Asian Studies* 11.3 (2012): 288–314.

Andersen, S. *The Enforcement of EU Law: The Role of the European Commission.* Oxford: Oxford University Press, 2012.

Andressen, M. "The evolving quality of trade between Canada and the United States." *Canadian Geographer* 52.1 (2008): 22–37.

Atkinson, A., T. Piketty and E. Saez. "Top incomes in the long run of history." *Journal of Economic Literature* 49 (2011): 3–71.

Autor, D., D. Dorn and G. Hanson. "The China syndrome: Local labor market effects of import competition in the United States." *American Economic Review* 103 (2013): 2121–68.

Baer, M.D. "North American free trade." *Foreign Affairs* 70.4 (1991): 132–49.

Bairoch, P. *Economics and World History.* Chicago: University of Chicago Press, 1993.

Balassa, B. *A "Stages" Approach to Comparative Advantage.* Washington, DC: International Bank for Reconstruction and Development, 1977.

Baldwin, R. *Globalization: The Great Unbundling(s).* Finland: Economic Council of Finland, 2006.

Barefoot, K. *U.S. Multinational Companies: Operations of U.S. Parents and their Foreign Affiliates in 2010.* Survey of Current Business, US Department of Commerce, 2012.

Barney, J.B. "Firm resources and sustained competitive advantage." *Journal of Management* 17 (1991): 99–120.

Barton, J.H., et al. *The Evolution of the Trade Regime*. Princeton: Princeton University Press, 2006.

BBC. "China's trade surplus jumps to $32bn." 12 February 2014.

Bell, M. and K. Pavitt. "Technological accumulation and industrial growth: contrasts between developed and developing countries." Archibugie, D. and J. Michie (eds.). *Technology, Globalisation and Economic Performance*. Cambridge: Cambridge University Press (1997): 83–137.

Bernard, A., J. Jensen and P. Schott. "Survival of the best fit." *Journal of International Economics* 68 (2006): 219–37.

Bhagwati, J.N. "Export-promoting trade strategies: issues and evidence." *World Bank Research Observer* 3.1 (1988): 27–57.

Birdsall, N., D. Rodrik and A. Subramanian. "How to help poor countries." *Foreign Affairs* 84 (2005): 136–52.

Blinder, A. "Offshoring: The next industrial revolution?" *Foreign Affairs* 45 (2006): 113.

Borjas, G., R. Freman and L. Katz. "On the labor market effects of immigration and trade." Borjas, G. and R. Freman (eds.). *Immigration and the Workforce*. Chicago: Chicago University Press (1992): 2133–44.

Bowen, H.V. *The Business of Empire: The East India Company and Imperial Britain*. Cambridge: Cambridge University Press, 2005.

Bowles, P. and B. MacLean. "Understanding trade bloc formation: The case of the ASEAN free trade area." *Review of International Political Economy* 3.2 (1993): 319–48.

Bramall, C. *Chinese Economic Development*. Abingdon: Routledge, 2009.

Burtless, G. "Workers' rights: Labor standards and global trade." *Brookings*. 1 September 2001.

Butlin, J. *Our Common Future*. London: Oxford University Press, 1989.

Carmody, P. *The New Scramble for Africa*. Cambridge: Polity Press, 2011.

Cattaneo, O., et al. *Assessing the Potential of Services in Trade in Developing Countries*. Washington, DC: World Bank, 2010.

CEPAL. *Global Value Chains and World Trade: Prospects and Challenges for Latin America*. Mexico City: Economic Commission for Latin America and the Caribbean, 2014.

Chalmers, D., G. Davies and G. Monti. *European Union Law: Cases and Texts*. Cambridge: Cambridge University Press, 2010.

Channel NewsAsia. Xi Offers China-driven "Asia Pacific Dream". Singapore, 9 November 2014.

Checkel, J.T. "International institutions and socialization in Europe: Introduction and framework." *International Organization* 59 (2005): 801–26.

China Daily. "Foxconn plans new plant to produce iPhone 7 touch-screen." 25 November 2014 (http://www.chinadaily.com.cn/regional/2014-11/25/content_18974896.htm, accessed 26 November 2014).

Cini, M. and N.P. Borragan. *European Union Politics*. Oxford: Oxford University Press, 2013.

Coase, R. "The nature of the firm." *Economica* 4 (1937): 386–405.

Coe, D. and E. Helpman. "International R&D spillovers." *European Economic Review* 39 (1995): 859–87.

Coe, N., et al. "Globalizing regional development: A global networks perspective." *Transactions of the Institute of British Geographers* 29 (2004): 468–84.

Coe, N.M. and H.W.C. Yeung. *Global Production Networks: Theorizing Economic Development in an Interconnected World*. Oxford: Oxford University Press, 2015.

Cohen, S. *Multinational Corporations and Foreign Direct Investment: Avoiding Simplicity, Embracing Complexity*. Oxford: Oxford University Press, 2007.

Cohen, W. and D. Levinthal. "Absorptive capacity: A new perspective on learning and innovation." *Adminstrative Science Quarterly* 35 (1990): 128–52.

Courchene, T.J. 2003. "FTA at 15, NAFTA at 10: A Canadian perspective on North American integration." *North American Journal of Economics and Finance* 14.3 (2003): 263–85.

Cowling, K. and P.R. Tomlinson. "The Japanese model in retrospect." *Policy Studies* 32 (2011): 569–83.

Dauvergne, P. *The Shadows of Consumption: Consequences for the Global Environment*. Cambridge: MIT Press, 2008.

Davis, S. and K. Caldeira. "Consumption-based accounting of CO_2 emissions." *Proceedings of the National Academy of Sciences* (2010): 5687–92.

Deardorff, A.V. and R.M. Stern. *Measurement of Non-Tariff Barriers*. Ann Arbor: University of Michigan Press, 1998.

Deardorff, A.V. and R.M. Stern. "What the public should know about globalization and the world trade organization." Research Seminar in International Economics. Discussion Paper Number 460. University of Michigan, Ann Arbor, 2000.

Decarlo, J. *Fair Trade and How it Works*. New York: Rosen Publishing, 2011.

Dicken, P. *Global Shift: Mapping the Changing Contours of the World Economy*. New York: Guilford Press, 2015.

Dinda, S. "Environmental Kuznets curve hypothesis: a survey." *Ecological Economics* 49 (2004): 431–55.

Donadiojune, R. "Britain's flight signals end of an era of transnational optimism." *New York Times*, 24 June 2016.

Doremus, P., et al. *The Myth of the Global Corporation*. Princeton: Princeton University Press, 1998.

Duhigg, C. and K. Bradsher. "How the U.S. lost out on iPhone work." 21 January 2012.

Dunning, J. "Explaining changing patterns of international production: In defense of the eclectic theory." *Oxford Bulletin of Economics and Statistics* 41 (1979): 269–96.

Economist, The. "Schools brief: The miracle of trade." 27 January 1996.

Economist, The. "Standing up to steel." 24 June 1999.

Economist, The. "The Hollow Men." 9 June 2012.

Economist, The. "Multinationals, it turns out, are evil after all." 11 September 2012.

Economist, The. "NAFTA at 20: Deeper, better NAFTA." 4 January 2014.

Elliott, K. and R. Freeman. *Can Labor Standards Improve Under Globalization?* Washington, DC: Peterson Institute Press, 2003.

Eurobarometer. *The European Constitution: Post-Referendum Survey in the Netherlands.* European Commission. Brussels, 2005.

Falvey, R., N. Foster and D. Greenaway. "North-south trade, knowledge spillovers and growth." *Journal of Economic Integration* 4 (2002): 650–70.

Farre, A. et al. "Commercial Arctic shipping through the Northeast Passage: Routes, resources, governance, technology and infrastracture." *Polar Geography* 37 (2014): 298–324.

Feenstra, R. and G. Hanson. "Globalization, outsourcing and wage inequality." *Papers and Proceedings of the 108th Meeting of the American Economic Association,* (1996): 240–45.

Feenstra, R. and G. Hanson. *Global Production Sharing and Rising Inequality: A Survey of Trade and Wages.* Washington, DC: NBER Working Paper 8372, 2001.

Forbes. "China leads in foreign direct investment." 5 November 2012.

Freeman, R. (1995) "Are your wages set in Beijing?" *The Journal of Economic Perspectives* 9: 15–32.

Fujita, M., I. Kuroiwa and S. Kumagai. *The Economics of East Asian Integration.* Cheltenham: Edward Elgar, 2011.

Gereffi, G., J. Humphrey and T. Sturgeon. "The governance of global value chains." *Review of International Political Economy* 12 (2005): 78–104.

Gereffi, G. and M. Korzeneiwicz (eds.) *Global Commodity Chains and Global Capitalism.* Westport: Praeger, 1994.

Glassman, J. "The geo-political economy of global production networks." *Geography Compass* 5 (2011): 154–65.

Glassman, J. and Y. Choi. "The chaebol and the US military industrial complex." *Environment and Planning A* 46 (2014): 1160–80.

Goldberg, P. and N. Pavcnik. "Distributional effects of globalization in developing countries." *Journal of Economic Literature* XLV (2007): 39–82.

Grossman, G. and E. Rossi-Hansberg. *The Rising of Offshoring: It's not Wine for Cloth Anymore.* Jackson Hole Conference Volume. Kansas City: Federal Reserve Bank, 2006.

Gunasegaram, P. "The problem with Proton." *The Star* 4 December 2010.

Hidalgo, C., K. Bailey, A-L. Barabási and R. Hausmann. "The product space conditions the development of nations." *Science* 317 (2007): 482–7.

Higgins, V. and J. Dibden. "Biosecurity, trade liberalization and the (anti) politics of risk analysis." *Environment and Planning A* 43 (2011): 393–409.

Hinkelman, E.G. *Dictionary of International Trade*. Novata, CA: World Trade Press, 2005.

Horner, R. "A new economic geography of trade and development?" *Territory, Politics and Governance* 4.4 (2015): 400–20.

Houssa, R. and M. Verpoorten. "The unintended consequence of an export ban." *World Development* 67 (2015): 138–50.

Hymer, S. *The International Operations of National Firms: A Study of Foreign Direct Investment*. Cambridge: MIT Press, 1976.

Jaffe, A. and M. Trajtenberg. "International knowledge flows: Evidence from patent citations." *Economics of Innovation and New Technology* 8 (1999): 105–36.

Johnson, C. *MITI and the Japanese Miracle*. Stanford: Stanford University Press, 1982.

Jonas, A.E.G. "Regions and place: Regionalism in question." *Progress in Human Geography* 36.2 (2012): 263–72.

Jordan, P.G. *Solar Energy Markets: An Analysis of the Global Solar Industry*. London: Elsevier, 2013.

Kahn, P. *The European Union*. New York: Infobase Publishing, 2008.

Kaplinsky, R. and M. Farooki. "What are the implications for global value chains when the market shifts from the north to the south?" *International Journal of Technological Learning* 4 (2011): 13–38.

Kemeny, T., D. Rigby and A. Cooke. "Cheap imports and the loss of US manufacturing jobs." *World Economy* 38 (2015): 1555–73.

Keohane, R. *After Hegemony: Cooperation and Discord in the World Political Economy*. Princeton: Princeton University Press, 1984.

Kim, S.Y. *Power and the Governance of Global Trade*. Ithaca: Cornell University Press, 2010.

Klasing, M. and P. Milinois. "Quantifying the evolution of world trade, 1870–1949". *Journal of International Economics* 92 (2014): 185–97.

Klein, M., C. Moser and D. Urban. *The Contribution of Trade to Wage Inequality: The Role of Skill, Gender and Nationality*. Washington, DC: NBER Working Paper No 15985, 2010.

Kletzer, L. *Imports, Exports and Jobs*. Kalmazoo: Upjohn Institute for Employment, 2002.

Kohl, T. and A.E. Brouwer. "The development of trade blocs in an era of globalization." *Environment and Planning A* 46 (2014): 1535–53.

Kravis, I.B. "Trade as a handmaiden of growth: Similarities between the nineteenth and twentieth centuries." *Economic Journal* 80 (1970): 850–72.

Krugman, P. "Myth of the Asian miracle." *Foreign Affairs* (1994): 62–78.

Kwabena, G.B. "Export instability and economic growth." *Economic Development and Cultural Change* 39 (1991): 815–28.

Laursen, F. "Introduction: Overview of the Constitutional Treaty and element of the Treaty." Laursen, F. (ed.). *The Rise and Fall of the EU's Constitutional Treaty*. Leiden: Martinus-Nijhoff Publisher, (2008): 1–25.

Lawrence, R. and M. Slaughter. *Trade and U.S. Wages: Great Sucking Sound or Small Hiccup?* Brooking Papers on Economic Activity, Macroeconomics. Washington, DC: Brookings Institution, 1993.

Lawrence, R.Z. "Japan's different trade regime: an analysis with particular reference to keiretsu." *Journal of Economic Perspectives* 7 (1993): 3–19.

Leontieff, W. "Domestic production and foreign trade: the American capital position re-examined." *Proceedings of the American Philosophical Society* 97.4 (1953): 332–49.

Lim, C.P. "Heavy industrialization: a second round of import-substitution." Jomo, K.S. (ed.). *Japan and Malaysian Development*. London: Routledge, (2001): 244–60.

Lockard, C. *Southeast Asia in World History*. New York: Oxford University Press, 2009.

Maddison, A. *The World Economy: A Millenial*. Paris: OECD, 2006.

Mantzavinos, C., D.C. North and S. Shariq. "Learning, institutions and economic performance." *Perspectives in Politics* 2 (2004): 75–84.

Marx, K. *Capital 3 Volumes*. New York: International, 1867.

Maskell, P. and A. Malmberg. "The competitiveness of firms and regions." *European Urban and Regional Studies* 6 (1999): 9–25.

McCann, G. "Ties that bind or binds that tie?" *Review of African Political Economy* (2010): 465–82.

McCormick, J. *Understanding the European Union: A Concise Introduction*. Basingstoke: Palgrave-MacMillan, 2014.

Mijiyawa, A.G. "Africa's recent economic growth: what are the contributing factors?" *African Development Review* 25 (2013): 289–302.

Mokyr, J. *The Gifts of Athena*. Princeton: Princeton University Press, 2002.

Mosley, L. and S. Uno. "Racing to the bottom or climbing to the top? Economic globalization and collective labor rights." *Comparative Political Studies* 40 (2007): 923–48.

Najam, A., M. Halle and L. Melendez-Ortiz (eds.) *Trade and Environment: A Resource Book*. IISD, 2007.

Navin, M.C. "Local food and international ethics." *Journal of Agricultural and Environmental Ethics* 27 (2014): 349–68.

Nolan, P. "China and the global business revolution". *Cambridge Journal of Economics* 26 (2002): 119–37.

North, D.C. *Institutions, Institutional Change and Economic Performance*. Cambridge: Cambridge University Press, 1990.

Ohmae, K. *The Borderless World*. New York: Free Press, 1990.

Pan, C. "What is Chinese about Chinese businesses?" *Journal of Contemporary China* 18 (2009): 7–25.

Peck, J. *Workplace: The Social Regulation of Labor Markets.* New York: Guilford Press, 1996.

Pena, C. and R. Rozemberg. *MERCOSUR: A Different Approach to Institutional Development.* Ottawa: FOCAL Policy Paper 05–06, 2005.

Pollan, M. *The Omnivore's Dilemma: A Natural History of Four Meals.* New York: Penguin, 2006.

Poon, J.P.H. "Exports, economic growth and development levels re-visited." *Journal of Economic Development* 20 (1995): 75–90.

Poon, J.P.H. "The cosmopolitanization of trade regions: global trends and implications." *Economic Geography* 73 (1997): 288–302.

Poon, J.P.H., E. Thompson and P. Kelly. "Myth of the triad? Geography of trade and investment blocs." *Transactions of the Institute of British Geographer* 25 (2000): 427–44.

Prebisch, R. "The economic development of Latin America and its principal problems." *Economic Bulletin for Latin America* 7 (1950): 1–22.

Qiang, Z., H. Sun, Y. Li, Y. Xu and J. Su. "China's solar photovoltaic policy: An analysis based on policy instruments." *Applied Energy* 129 (2014): 308–19.

Reid, A. *Southeast Asia in the Age of Commerce, 1450–1680.* New Haven, CT: Yale University Press, 1988.

Ricardo, D. *On the Principles of Political Economy and Taxation.* London: John-Murray, 1817.

Richards, D. "Trade-related intellectual property rights." *Review of International Political Economy* 12 (2005): 535–51.

Rigby, D. and S. Breau. "Impacts of trade on wage inequality in Los Angeles." *Annals of the Association of American Geographers* 98 (2008): 920–40.

Ruggie, G. *Constructing the World Polity: Essays on International Institutions.* Abingdon: Routledge, 1998.

Salem, S. and F. Rozental. "Labor standards and trade: A review of recent empirical evidence." *Journal of International Commerce and Economics* (2012): 63–98.

Sawkut, R., S. Vinesh and F. Sooraj. "The net contribution of the Mauritian export processing zone using benefit–cost analysis." *Journal of International Development* 21 (2009): 379–92.

Saxenian, A. *The New Arganauts: Regional Advantage in a Global Economy.* Cambridge: Cambridge University Press, 2007.

Selznick, P. "Institutionalism 'old' and 'new'." *Adminstrative Science Quarterly* 41 (1996): 270–77.

Sheppard, E. "Constructing free trade: from Manchester boosterism to global management." *Transactions of the Institute of British Geographers* (2005): 151–72.

Sheridan, B.J. "Manufacturing exports and growth: when is a developing country ready to transition from primary exports to manufacturing exports?" *Journal of Macroeconomics* 42 (2014): 1–13.

Singer, H. "Terms of trade and economic development." Eatwell, J., Milgate, M. and Newman, P. (eds.). *The New Palgrave Dictionary of Economics*. London: MacMillan, 1987.

Smith, A. *An Inquiry into the Nature and Causes of the Wealth of Nations*. London: Strahan and Cadell, 1776.

Soble, J. "Failure of Obama's trade deal could hurt US influence in Asia." *New York Times* (2015).

Stanwick, P. and S. Stanwick. *Understanding Business Ethics*. Thousand Oaks: Sage, 2016.

Stiles, K. "Negotiating institutional reform: The Uruguay Round, the GATT and the WTO." *Global Governance* 2 (1996): 119–48.

Sturgeon, T. "How do we define value chains and production networks?" *Institute of Development Studies Bulletin* 32 (2001): 9–18.

Tinbergen, J. *Shaping the World Economy*. New York: Twentieth Century Fund, 1962.

TNS Opinion & Social. *International Trade*. Eurobarometer 357. Brussels: European Commission, 2010.

Trindale, V. "The big push, industrialization and international trade: The role of exports." *Journal of Development Economics* 78 (2005): 22–48.

Tyson, L.D. *Who's Bashing Whom? Trade Conflict in High-Technology Industries*. Washington, DC: Institute for International Economics, 1992.

UNCTAD. *World Investment Report: Transnational Corporations, Market Structure and Competition*. New York: United Nations, 1997.

UNCTAD. *World Investment Report 2004: The Shift towards Services*. Geneva: United Nations, 2004.

UNCTAD. *World Investment Report: Transnational Corporations, Agricultural Production and Development*. New York: United Nations, 2009.

UNCTAD. *Intellectual Property in the World Trade Organization*. New York: United Nations, 2010.

UNCTAD. *World Investment Report: Non-equity Modes of International Production and Development*. Geneva: United Nations, 2011a.

UNCTAD. *Commodities at a Glance*. Geneva: United Nations, 2011b.

UNCTAD. *Global Value Chains, Investment and Trade for Development*. Geneva: United Nations, 2013a.

UNCTAD. *Economic Development in Africa Report*. Geneva: United Nations, 2013b.

UNCTAD. "Studies in technology transfer." *UNCTAD Current Studies on Science, Technology and Innovation*. Geneva: United Nations, 2014a.

UNCTAD. "Transfer of technology and knowledge sharing for development." *UNCTAD Current Studies on Science, Technology and Innovation*. Geneva: United Nations, 2014b.

UNCTAD. *World Investment Report 2015*. Geneva: United Nations, 2015.

UNHDR. *United Nations Human Development Report: The Rise of the South*. New York: United Nations, 2013.

Verhoogen, E. "Trade, quality upgrading and wage inequality in the Mexican manufacturing sector." *Quarterly Journal of Economics* 132 (2008): 489–531.

Villarreal, M.A. and I.F. Fergusson. "Nafta at 20: overview and trade effects." *CRS Report*. Library of Congress, 2014.

Wallerstein, I. *World-Systems Analysis: An Introduction*. Durham: Duke University Press, 2004.

Watson, W.G. "North American free trade: lessons from the trade data." *Canadian Public Policy* 28 (1992): 1–12.

Werner, M. *Global Displacements: The Making of Uneven Development in the Caribbean*. Oxford: Wiley-Blackwell, 2016.

Wilkins, M. "The history of multinational enterprise". Rugman, A. and Brewer, T. (eds.). *Oxford Handbook of International Business*. Oxford: Oxford University Press, 2001.

Williamson, J.G. *Trade and Poverty: When the Third World Fell Behind*. Cambridge: MIT Press, 2011.

World Bank. *The East Asian Miracle*. Washington, DC, 1993.

World Bank. *Special Economic Zone: Performance, Lessons Learned and Implications for Zone Development*. Washington, DC, 2008.

WTO. *World Trade Report 2008: Trade in a Globalizing World*. Geneva: World Trade Organization, 2008.

WTO. *International Trade Statistics*. Geneva: World Trade Organization, 2013.

Xing, Y. and N. Detert. *How the iPhone Widens the United States Trade Deficit with the People's Republic of China*. Working Paper #257. Manila: Asian Development Bank, 2010.

Yeung, H.W.C. *Strategic Coupling: East Asian Industrial Transformation in The New Global Economy*. Ithaca: Cornell University Press, 2016.

Yonekura, S. and S. McKinney. "Innovative multinational firms: Japan as a case study". Chandler, A. and Mazlish, B. (eds.). *Leviathans: Multinational Corporation and the New Global History*. Cambridge: Cambridge University Press, 2005.

Yoshimatsu, H. "US-East Asian trade friction: exit and voice in the steel trade regime." *Asian Affairs* 30 (2003): 200–17.

INDEX

Numbers in **bold** indicate tables, *italics* indicates figures.

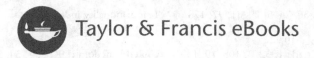

Taylor & Francis eBooks

Helping you to choose the right eBooks for your Library

Add Routledge titles to your library's digital collection today. Taylor and Francis ebooks contains over 50,000 titles in the Humanities, Social Sciences, Behavioural Sciences, Built Environment and Law.

Choose from a range of subject packages or create your own!

Benefits for you

» Free MARC records
» COUNTER-compliant usage statistics
» Flexible purchase and pricing options
» All titles DRM-free.

Benefits for your user

» Off-site, anytime access via Athens or referring URL
» Print or copy pages or chapters
» Full content search
» Bookmark, highlight and annotate text
» Access to thousands of pages of quality research at the click of a button.

REQUEST YOUR FREE INSTITUTIONAL TRIAL TODAY

Free Trials Available
We offer free trials to qualifying academic, corporate and government customers.

eCollections – Choose from over 30 subject eCollections, including:

Archaeology	Language Learning
Architecture	Law
Asian Studies	Literature
Business & Management	Media & Communication
Classical Studies	Middle East Studies
Construction	Music
Creative & Media Arts	Philosophy
Criminology & Criminal Justice	Planning
Economics	Politics
Education	Psychology & Mental Health
Energy	Religion
Engineering	Security
English Language & Linguistics	Social Work
Environment & Sustainability	Sociology
Geography	Sport
Health Studies	Theatre & Performance
History	Tourism, Hospitality & Events

For more information, pricing enquiries or to order a free trial, please contact your local sales team:
www.tandfebooks.com/page/sales

Routledge
Taylor & Francis Group

The home of
Routledge books

www.tandfebooks.com